By William Norman Mitchell

For all who wear the label of executive, those with years of experience and those on the way up, this book promises to become a classic.

From a vast background of knowledge gained working with many of America's leading business organizations, the author analyzes such vital issues as the true role of the executive, the source and use of his power, the prime factors that motivate his performance, and the steps he must take to insure both his own and his company's future success.

The main elements of the executive job are thoroughly examined, and the problems of compensation, the quest for permanence, and the development of future managerial talent are frankly discussed. Valuable suggestions are given for company growth and accomplishments through effective executive recruiting, and candid advice is offered to those young executives who are striving to broaden their business careers.

Here is an enlightening appraisal of the executive job and of the new responsibilities that face the men who practice its skills.

William Norman Mitchell is a partner in the management consulting firm of A. T. Kearney & Company. For more than 38 years he has worked with leading government agencies, technical societies, and a distinguished cross-section of private business enterprises on organizational and policy matters. He was formerly Professor of Business Organization at the University of Chicago, and served as Associate Dean of the School of Business.

The Business
Executive
in a
Changing World

The Business
Executive
in a
Changing World

WILLIAM NORMAN MITCHELL

AMERICAN MANAGEMENT ASSOCIATION

To
S. B. M.
whose moral support
has never failed me

Contents

Introduction

TO UNDERTAKE THE WRITING OF A BOOK—ESPECIALLY A BUSINESS
book addressed specifically to a sophisticated managerial audience—obligates one, I suspect, first to consider four quite fundamental questions:
1. *Why* should the project be undertaken at all?
2. *Who* may possibly be interested?
3. *What* are to be the underlying assumptions—the special
   frame of reference providing limits for the proposed
   discussion?
4. *How* can the discussion best be organized to attract the
   prospective reader's notice?

That the problem of management in today's environment is
of first-rate concern to businessmen will be readily granted. The
chief executive of a very successful enterprise recently declared,
for instance, that in his business as in many others, "money
was once our prime problem." But, thanks to "good times,"
almost any project with a promising future can now find adequate financial backing. In his estimation, "what instead represents the top problem of today's business is executive manpower
and how to organize available human effort."

Few thoughtful executives will quarrel with this general order
of priorities assigned to present-day business problems.

The critical nature of the executive manpower problem has
recently been bluntly emphasized by the influential Committee

on Economic Development (CED) in the warning that "good young executives are scarce and going to get even scarcer unless managements bestir themselves in more effective efforts to fill this gap." It is, furthermore, a disconcerting coincidence that paralleling this admonishment in business circles to try harder to develop better executives there should also be insistent rumors in educational circles that the prospect of an executive career is progressively less appealing. Placement officers in good universities have been asserting that their best graduates are tending more and more to seek careers in law, in science, in the "creative" arts, in public service, and in teaching instead of in business, which hitherto has had a steady appeal for college graduates.

This trend—if indeed it is a trend—is especially regrettable when, as is also persistently reported, there are on university campuses growing feelings of scorn for business as a career, especially among superior students who possibly reflect the attitudes of teachers they most admire. Business, they reportedly believe, is "an intellectual wasteland fit only for money-grubbing conformists"!

Hasty vocational appraisals and comparisons may conceivably be dismissed as the idealistic imaginings of the very young and inexperienced. They really are signs of the provincialism to which "intellectuals" unfortunately sometimes seem no more immune than the ordinary man. In the long run, this uncomplimentary verdict very likely is self-correcting since the social utility of any career, whether that of an artist, a scientist, an educator, or an administrator, clearly depends more upon the man than upon his vocation. Every man who wins lasting social approval is essentially a "teacher" in any event.

But business leaders, always on the lookout for good recruits, clearly ought not to permit this biased view to go unchallenged. It is squarely up to them to demonstrate that the role of business executives in a free society can be as rigorous and intellectually exciting as young men with superior minds may wish.

The critical dimensions of the executive replacement problem confronting modern business are readily stated. There are today in American business firms, it has been estimated, something like 200,000 top executive positions. Each of these is occupied by someone who must be replaced within a few short years. Doubtless some of them, because of change and the resulting confusion, sheer mental laziness, lack of intelligent direction, or the mere fact that they have stopped growing, will unfortunately become inadequate before their time. All of them will with the utmost certainty be compelled eventually to surrender to the call of advancing age.

The sources of suitable replacements can also be reduced to reasonably accurate quantitative terms. Liberal arts colleges, engineering schools, and business schools turn out each year a combined total of graduates numbering well up in six figures. Despite the personal preferences which some of the more promising liberal arts graduates are reported to entertain, large numbers from all three sources will always look forward to careers in business, and some fairly predictable proportion of this total can be expected eventually to become competent executives.

How soon after selection those who show promise can be made ready for important executive responsibilities inevitably depends upon both employer and employee. Men with potential always need encouragement and assistance in working out a systematic program of self-improvement. Opportunities for broadened experience must be created by deliberately moving them as frequently as practicable from one challenging assignment to another. Risks of overspecialization in some inherently attractive technical job must be avoided. Above all, each candidate must make his own education a continuing process.

This crucial business problem has not, of course, gone unnoticed. The American Management Association and kindred organizations are untiring in efforts to supplement the in-plant management training processes of business.

That a great deal is being written on the subject also is obvious. Published materials, of more than passing interest, which have appeared in the past five years or so fill an eight-foot bookshelf quite amply. The list includes approximately 300 items of book or shorter length with a total of something like 20,000 printed pages!

The majority of these selected writings deal with the "middle management" level—occupied in most part by "technical specialists'' in the executive group. They are replete with discussions of "how to" solve the problems with which staff men deal in every business and liberally interlarded with case materials describing solutions to these problems which have been discovered by others.

This exceedingly practical emphasis is not surprising. The need for skilled specialists in support of modern management is very great and amazingly diverse. Today's problems require expert treatment but are often assigned to subordinates who are none too resourceful, experienced, or prepared for what they are supposed to do. This is the segment of management, furthermore, where "teaching by example" is likely to yield most easily measured returns.

Truly impressive efforts to train the "specialists" in business management possibly have outstripped equally essential efforts respecting the "generalists" in management—those occupying the top echelons in the executive structure. Certainly the need for competence at this strategic level is equally great. A dearth of adequate replacements from within when the need for making top-level changes does arrive, manifestly, is all too common. Hence the general manager, at whatever level he happens to operate, is the specific target in this discussion.

General executives require very special credentials. Extraordinary talents, discovered by systematic selection procedures and nurtured by carefully guided experience, are essential to achieve a position of unquestioned leadership in voluntary associations of free men. Executive success depends upon a thorough understanding of the nature and limits of executive authority and of the functions which executives must perform in an intensely competitive environment. It requires that a man know how executive efforts are best organized; how order is established in operations; which are the motivations that men in varied circumstances seem most likely to respond to; and how permanence in the midst of change—the fundamental goal of all institutions—can be assured in the private business firm. It demands a knowledge of the distinctive setting of the executive's characteristic role and of the means by which he may prepare himself to play this role with credit.

These are the elements which give form and challenge to every executive's career. To understand this career, the general bill of particulars just cited should, I suspect, be examined in about the order mentioned. The table of contents which follows these introductory remarks closely parallels this listing.

It is the purpose of this discussion to identify important generalizations of use in developing capable top executives—tough-minded always, in enforcing internal efficiency; scrupulous also, in doing their best to help preserve a vigorous and free market economy. For enlightened managers as members of the business community can no more afford to neglect the second of these responsibilities than they can the first. Free enterprise is a concept with which nearly everyone in our particular society agrees in principle but which, alas, seems continually in danger of being gradually whittled away by ill-considered public and selfish private actions.

This is not a case study recording the experiences of any particular business organization. It is based instead upon good fortune over many years in observing at first hand, as it were, what contributes to continuing success—or chronic failure—in the typical business firm.

To engage in a project of this sort is to incur, inevitably, many obligations for which warm thanks are due: Miss Kathleen Nee and Miss Virginia Thatcher have provided skilled secretarial and editorial services in fitting this manuscript for publication. Their conscientious and expert assistance is much appreciated and sincerely acknowledged, as is the help of AMA's editorial staff.

Several friends whose judgment I greatly value have generously consented to read the manuscript as it has gradually evolved. They have made indispensable contributions to its improvement. Among these, Mrs. Barbara Wendell Kerr deserves special mention. Her obvious competence in journalistic fields, with which I myself have but slight familiarity, made her constructive suggestions concerning my efforts especially helpful in the early stages of this undertaking. I am greatly indebted to her and to two of my partners in particular, Stuart Files and Lee Wendell, who have generously given similar assistance.

Harry Dreiser, Editor of Publications, and Professors James Lorie and Edward Wrapp, all of the Graduate School of Business, University of Chicago, have encouraged me to complete the project by offering helpful observations for which I am grateful.

The content and organization of that which follows are, of course, my own, and I take full responsibility for them—though who can say what particular associations over a lifetime have influenced one's own convictions? I wish, in fact, to acknowledge a very special indebtedness in this particular connection to three specific groups:

1. To my partners and associates in the firm of A. T. Kearney & Company, Inc., Management Consultants, whose counsel these many years has been invaluable to me.

2. To literally hundreds of students in executive training whose paths have crossed my own, who have so often turned out to be my teachers, and who in unnumbered instances today occupy positions of trust in American business.

3. To a host of clients who year after year have generously shared their business experiences and problems with me and who sometimes, in critical matters, have even paid me the heartwarming compliment of listening to my advice.

To this company of friends, and others of like mind, this book is in particular addressed. It is my hope that among them there may be readers who find in these pages something of value, reflecting some stray beams of light from facets of their own rich experience in the practice of the executive arts.

—W. N. MITCHELL
Chicago, Illinois

I

The Executive's Credentials

THE DISTINGUISHING CREDENTIAL OF THE EXECUTIVE GROUP IN ANY OR-
ganization is possession of authority sufficient for whatever the
occasion requires. This special identification implies the "right"
or "power" to take command and perform the functions of
management in the organization's affairs.

But this right is never securely established—at least in any
voluntary association—by unilateral determination. Democratic
institutions depend upon the consent of those who sponsor them,
identified in various ways as members, communicants, incor-
porators, donors, citizens, owners, or whatever designation may
seem appropriate under the circumstances. The internal sanctions which they provide are naturally subordinate to the external authority (or authorities) under which voluntary and private groups are suffered to exist.

It is characteristic of executive authority, despite this internal
mandate, that it cannot rise above its ulterior source. Authorized leaders in any organization must make sure of the reliability of this external bench mark, the validity of the credentials
they derive from it, and the precise limits within which they
must operate.

The sense of direction which leaders acquire within these external limits depends upon acceptance by their followers. But
the presence of numbers in any group activity, including many

who very likely harbor pronounced feelings of individual importance, requires that those authorized to lead be articulate and
capable of inspiring confidence. They must exercise their prerogatives with self-assurance and a suitable show of dignity and
decorum through regularly established custom and procedure.

Private Enterprise Based on Property Rights

Business executives operate within the confines of some private business firm and are inevitably preoccupied with the
human, economic, and technological problems of that particular
firm. All these problems in one way or another conspire to lay
great emphasis upon property. Recognition that it is the prime
business of the state to protect human rights—including quite
specifically, among others, the right to own property—has always been a cornerstone of Western political thought.

Shallow clichés which attempt to make distinctions between
"human rights" and "property rights," as though the latter
were relatively somewhat tainted, clearly represent a play on
words of no real meaning. It is a distinction which would have
made little sense to an earlier generation of pioneers, as indeed
it does to men of this generation who increasingly have enjoyed,
at first hand, the satisfactions experienced by "men of property." Actually, there is little point in attempting to rank the
various human rights or freedoms in an arbitrary scale of
values. All of them are bound to stand or fall together.

The very essence of the institution of private property is that
ownership carries with it the right to control and determine the
use to which property is to be put. It implies freedom to place
one's holdings at risk, if one so desires, and to enjoy the fruits
thereof. No responsible person questions the fact that the right
of ownership carries with it certain quite specific obligations,
just as other human rights do, but these are the precautions
ordinarily imposed by a free society to insure the equitable protection of all its members.

The legitimate line of managerial authority in the private
business firm is thus from the state to the owners to chosen
intermediaries to the office of the chief executive.

The Corporate Structure of Enterprise

This franchise is restricted and specified by law, for what the state gives it obviously may take away. Owners in turn, by acts of delegation, similarly limit the authority of their agents if by chance they do not themselves elect to manage their affairs directly. The simple and essentially informal owner-manager relationships observed in individual proprietorships and partnerships serve well enough in small and highly personal business undertakings. These ordinarily must give way to more adaptable corporate devices as operations grow and take on increasing complexity.

Few inventions of modern times have influenced the economic affairs of the Western World more profoundly than the concept of the corporation. It is free society's prime means of organizing production. It provides the essential framework for widespread private ownership of material resources. It facilitates capital mobilization in aggregates consistent with modern needs. It protects contributing owners in the exercise of their natural property rights.

The legal fiction of a corporate personality is a great organizational convenience which makes continuing institutional existence possible. There is no longer need for dependence upon the tenure of those individuals who at any given moment represent its substance. The owners or their executive agents retire from action one by one, with no particular claim to indispensability, but the corporate body, granted useful goals and adjustment to changing circumstances, can apparently endure without end. This corporate quality of permanence is unquestionably a much-needed stabilizer in a privately controlled industrial society.

The well-nigh insatiable technological demands for capital and the extreme measures necessary to meet these requirements in present-day corporate enterprise need little by way of documentation. Our 500 largest industrial corporations, for example, represent capital accumulations in dollar amounts well above 100 billion. The vast army of stockholders who have provided this great reservoir of net worth includes more than 11 million persons. Their number is, in fact, more than one and one-half times the number of employees.

Extremely diversified and necessarily impersonal corporate ownership of these general dimensions would scarcely be practicable were it not that corporate equities can be made highly attractive to participating investors. Because incorporation implies the creation of a synthetic personality, acts performed in the corporate name are generally interpreted as its own, and titles to ownership can be passed from investor to investor with almost complete freedom.

The Prime Risk Takers

Stockholders are the ultimate "insiders" in this corporate complex. Their privileges of participation and the authority they wield conform, at least in substance, with accepted concepts and rights of property ownership. Their corresponding obligations as corporate owners and "common stockholders" are bound up with the fact that they are the residual risk takers. The role of venture capital as the underlying stimulus to innovation, a major virtue of private capitalism, requires this.

But how can a healthy appetite for risk taking be stimulated among these investors?

The uncoveted position as prime risk takers in which stockholders find themselves among the various self-serving groups comprising the private firm calls for some compensatory grant of special powers and privileges. Otherwise, this burden would very likely be totally devoid of attraction to potential "volunteers" among investors. He who is sure to lose when things go wrong must be in a position to gain when things go well, or there will be no takers.

When economic circumstances or ill-advised public action, encouraged by popular misunderstanding, places this hope of gain in jeopardy, the sources of venture capital are sure to dry up. Some built-in assurance respecting risks and profits must, in consequence, be available to hapless stockholders, lest they too, when reminded of the consequences of their misfortunes and misjudgments, develop a reluctance to take chances.

Personal cravings for security, though understandable, clearly have no real place in an enterprise system either for owners or for whomever they choose to represent them. It is not the function of government to be always ready to raise a protective umbrella over every untried private venture destined to turn out badly, but neither can the agencies of government remain indifferent when private assumption of business risk is discouraged through lack of profit incentives. Private enterprise depends upon this form of nourishment.

Special encouragements to private corporate investors to assume a vital role as risk takers in our economy include three very significant provisions:

1. Stockholders fall heir to whatever is left of corporate income when all contractual claims have been met.
2. Stockholders have, collectively, the determining voice in the investment policies of the firm, even though they may neither individually nor collectively be able to implement these policies. This privilege of common stockholders may indeed seem tenuous in huge modern corporations, but through collective action it remains inviolate regardless of size. Like individual voters in a democracy, stockholders have only to find means of asserting themselves to be effective.
3. Personal immunity absolving stockholders from blame for acts of their corporate creation, and limitation of their losses, should these occur, to the amount they have invested in the firm, constitute a substantial quid pro quo for the necessary surrender of their rights of direct management to designated representatives.

Delegation as an Administrative Necessity

It is true that exercise of these basic rights and privileges of corporate ownership can be achieved only through an orderly process of delegation. This is an administrative necessity in large and impersonal aggregations of joint owners embracing extremely diverse individual aims and interests.

In more personal nonchartered individual proprietorships and partnerships, direct management by owners is much more feasible. In these less formal organizations, furthermore, owners have no special immunities. One joint owner, unless expressly limited by deliberate public notice, may even bind his associates by contractual agreements with third parties whether known or unknown to them. Several joint owners, acting among themselves for mutual convenience, may delegate management responsibilities to others possessing no vested ownership. But, lacking the immunity afforded corporate stockholders, they are likely for their own protection to be much more personally and directly participants in management.

This contrasting position of corporate stockholders is of great significance. It has served to introduce into corporate affairs great flexibility in financial transactions. But—even more important in terms of executive status—it has contributed an institutional climate friendly to the growth of a managerial class possessing truly professional instincts.

It seems not improbable that this favored group may come eventually to possess the expertise and occupational solidarity consistent with the changing requirements of private business in a free society. Already there is ample evidence that, in this executive élite, eligibility for recognition depends in major degree upon individual ability. This is surely a much more significant qualification for executive preferment than mere demonstrated success in accumulating or, with even less relevance, falling heir to personal wealth.

These necessary restrictions upon freedom of stockholder action are not in fact especially burdensome. The implied concept of property ownership that "to own carries with it the right and privilege to control" is still valid. Stockholders as a group, though the group's composition may be continually changing, always have the final voice in determining what shall be done.

Always, however, this final voice is a group possession capable of implementation only through acts of election and delegation. The transitory nature of some stockholders' tenure, the lack of individual competence or articulate interest, the fact that there may be great numbers of stockholders unknown to each other, the basic difficulty of the individual in getting his own voice of authority heard in the babel of conflicting voices—all these make impractical any recourse other than delegation.

Strategic Role of the Board of Directors

In corporate practice precise rules and restrictions govern the way in which stockholders exercise their authority through representatives, ostensibly of their own number and choosing, who thus act as their agents. It is assumed that these representatives will be better equipped than the owners in the aggregate to establish order and maintain efficiency.

The board of directors is the intermediary mechanism which, collectively, functions as go-between for the owners and the executive hierarchy. The board's duties in this chain of command, its natural limitations, its manner of organization, and the prerogatives which it chooses to assume or relinquish, affect the credentials of the executives profoundly and quite definitely set the pattern of executive behavior. It is for this reason essential at this point in our discussion that the board's proper functions and characteristic methods of operation be examined in detail.

There are always insurmountable difficulties in vesting day-to-day administrative authority in the board as such, for in this capacity it is scarcely better equipped for the task than are the stockholders themselves. Frequently, it must be of considerable size if it is to provide representation for all significant shades of ownership desires. The board, like its owner principals, must arrive at official decisions through group action, not as individuals; and the intermittent schedule on which the members meet for deliberation hampers forthright action still further. In consequence, the board must choose still other agencies that can act in truly executive capacities.

Charter and bylaw stipulations place explicit restrictions on the subject areas in which boards are deemed competent and permitted official independence of action. Some areas are allotted exclusively to it; some are subject to stockholder ratification; many, especially those pertaining to operations, are—by

custom and general amenity, if not by legal requirement—
reserved to the office of the chief executive.

The board's mandate is not of itself limited in any very
oppressive way by these restrictions. It may, in fact, exercise
extraordinary power in corporate government provided it be-
stirs itself. Its members, both as a formal body and as individual members (even though, in the latter case, they have no
official authority), can provide invaluable support to the chief
executive as mentors, counselors, and critics.

Directors by intent are clearly expected to be more than
figureheads or rubber stamps for management. True, they may
hardly be counted upon to be more than this if dominated by the
octogenarian complaisance of superannuated members on
whom a final honor has been bestowed at the close of an active
business career. And their influence may be even worse if, instead, they are dominated by vociferous stockholder minorities
bent on having their own way.

The crucial problem is to secure men who are both competent
and interested. Though presumably chosen by stockholders
acting as an organized electorate, in practice the choice frequently rests with the chief executive instead. There are few
responsibilities that he should take more seriously, provided he
is in a position to influence the selection of directors; for his task
and lot, by their very nature, create a distinct craving and need
for objective advisers.

Executive Authority Not a Duplication of Board Authority

The underlying theory respecting the division of authority
between the board and subordinate management is that the
latter should be charged quite explicitly with results. Defining
desired ends is the natural prerogative of a board alert to its
responsibilities, but choice of means ought always to be an executive prerogative.

These distinctions, though seldom honored precisely in practice, cannot be dismissed as artificial or arbitrary. Reasonable
observance of them, in fact, provides the only rational way of
allocating powers between directorate and executive authority.

Without this observance, their different functions fade into one another and are lost in noxious duplication of effort and general confusion.

The directorate, even as it assumes from stockholders the primary task of government in the corporate entity, must itself distinguish quite positively between its own functions and those of the executive hierarchy. The boundary is an entirely proper and important one, although actually, in terms of specific cases, it is one of degree rather than of objectives or subject matter. Neither the board nor its committees (which rarely are empowered to act solely on their own in that their conclusions must be ratified by the full board) can be effective in executing corporate policy. But within its natural limitations the board should, nevertheless, be a working body.

Directors must understand that they serve in the capacity of trustees, accepting the customary obligations and personal liabilities attendant upon trusteeship. They are expected to establish a consensus of the owners' wishes and interests and to interpret these to management; to give counsel; to set guidelines for objectives and policies; to evaluate results; and, in extremity and usually with great reluctance, to apply corrective discipline. On the rare occasions where the board takes direct action on its own initiative to conserve corporate and ownership interest, to decide the disposition of earnings, or to dismiss corporate officers, it is exercising its indispensable disciplinary prerogatives. There are no proper substitutes for it in these matters.

Clearer recognition and stricter observance of this basic role of the directorate would serve to expose the fallacy inherent in setting up boards predominantly composed of partisan representatives of either self-centered ownership interests or inside management. In modern "publicly owned" corporations, large ownership interests are not very typical among either directors or managers; however, the prevalence of directors with negligible personal ownership can lead to erroneous conclusions, for the personal influence of an individual board member for good or ill sometimes depends in actual fact not so much upon the magnitude of his own investment as upon his representation by proxy of powerful ownership interests. Should these have been acquired under other corporate auspices for the very purpose of

manipulating to their own advantage the affairs of the organization which the board member supposedly serves, he is almost
inevitably confronted, sooner or later, by overwhelming conflicts
of interest.

Intercorporate ownership arrangements of this sort ought
always to be subject to public surveillance, not because they are
wrong per se, but because they create personal temptations to
indulge in serious competitive abuses. Ulterior corporate motives for stock ownership implemented by interlocking director-
ships serving to hamper a firm's freedom of action in its own
interests are manifestly bad, for they strike at the very root of
the system depended upon to preserve the inherent right of all
firms to independence.

But the common practice of permitting the board to become
heavily loaded with representatives of management probably is
of even greater significance in determining how this primary
ruling body actually functions. In more than one-half of this
country's 500 largest industrial companies, for instance, the
board includes a majority of inside or management members.
Even among those currently classed as outside members there is
a liberal sprinkling of men who achieved board membership before retirement from active management. In less than one-
fourth of this group of large companies is the proportion of
truly outside members sufficient to place them in a position to
dominate the deliberations of the board without question.

If it is logical to contend that boards of directors have unique
and specific functions to perform, it hardly makes sense to give
predominance to management representatives. The board's responsibilities are quickly obscured under this type of domina-
tion. At best, its deliberations are prone to duplicate an order of
business which might be appropriate to a management committee.
At worst, the chief executive officer is placed in the untenable
position of being subject to the direction of his subordinates in
management who are also board members. Either he dominates
them, defeating the unique functions of the board, or they dominate him.

Anyone who has witnessed a palace revolt in which management members of the board have brazenly demanded the ouster
of their chief executive officer can well appreciate the unhappy

consequences of these proceedings. There manifestly are occasions when chief executives should be called strictly to account, but decisions to do so should be based upon objective judgments. Personal rivalries, disappointed ambitions, and incompatibility of temperament are not compelling reasons.

Selection and Internal Organization of the Board

This unnatural balance of power within the board obviously cannot be corrected unless good outside directors can be found in sufficient numbers. They must be selected from executives or men of experience in business affairs—preferably, perhaps, though not necessarily with a large personal investment in the company—who can and are willing to make a real contribution to its affairs.

Members of the banking and legal professions often are chosen because their special experience is useful to the board, though their presence may sometimes prove embarrassing when their associates would prefer to seek financial or legal services elsewhere. The judgment of such representatives is sometimes less forthright than is required when their obligations as corporate directors conflict with their other, more impelling business or professional interests. "Banker control" of corporate policy may indeed create its own problems.

It has frequently been contended that boards of directors should have a more liberal representation from the nonexecutive professions with no special or selfish interest to promote. Perhaps an economist, an engineer or physical scientist, a retired military or naval officer with special aptitudes, a specialist in organization or industrial relations, or a distinctly public-minded member of whatever background can make a valuable impact upon the board's thinking.

The important criterion is that all members be chosen primarily for their individual potential for contribution rather than because they represent some particular interest. Official representatives of labor, of government, of consumers, and—least of all—of suppliers or competitors have no place on corporate boards if their connections are the reason for their choice. All these interests as well as ownership are vital to the conduct of corporate business, but in the free enterprise system they have their own devices outside of board membership for making their influence felt. The board, like executive management, ought to be inspired above all else by the long-run interests, in the broadest sense, of the firm itself.

Men who have pronounced acquisitive instincts as expressed in getting themselves elected to boards of directors should by all means be avoided. Most individuals who have more than three or four memberships on important boards to which they give more than perfunctory service soon find their attention so scattered that they cannot make an outstanding contribution to any of them. The board member's motivation should be something stronger than personal vanity. True, the basic reason for consenting to share the responsibility for a firm's future may in most cases be more a matter of status than of financial compensation, but it is clear, nevertheless, that if outside directors are to be secured who meet the desired qualifications, the problems of motivation, financial and otherwise, should not be dealt with casually. Competent directors are as worthy of their hire as are competent executives.

Whether the chairman of the board is primarily concerned with acting as presiding officer and is therefore a corporate figurehead, whether he serves in addition as chief executive officer, or whether instead both functions are the combined responsibility of the president appears usually to reflect an adjustment to local conditions and personalities. It is essential in any event, for the sake of promoting effective internal communications, that the chief executive officer be a full-fledged board member.

The division of labor between board and chief executive ought always to be justified by the same test applied to all divisions of labor. Duplication of effort must be avoided. Just as the board, acting in its capacity as a corporate ruling body, must recognize its practical limitations and confine its efforts to its particular functions, there must be equally explicit operational distinctions throughout the structure of management beneath. Each level in the hierarchy must justify its existence and validate its credentials by performing some unique function. Otherwise, there are bound to be frustration and wasted executive effort.

*   *   *

In brief, then, the system of executive authority centered in the office of the chief executive traces its lineage and official credentials unmistakably through clearly defined channels. The progression, once more, is as follows:

1. From the *state* as the external authority under which such voluntary and private groups as the modern corporation exist;
2. To the *corporate* owners, or stockholders, serving as the prime risk takers;
3. To the *members of the board,* representing the owners and acting for them in the role of trusteeship;
4. To the *chief executive and his subordinate managers,* charged with responsibility for operating results under the direction of the board as mentors, counselors, and critics.

Without the respected status this unquestionable legitimacy affords, this essential power center could scarcely be established or long endure.

II

The Anatomy of Executive Leadership

THE BUSINESS EXECUTIVE'S AUTHORITY IS ALWAYS COUNTERBALANCED by a heavy burden of responsibility. In our system of private enterprise, the welfare of individual firms as a group is closely bound up with the welfare of the system. There can be no general prosperity on the one side unless those on the other side also prosper. Executives with a conscience and a proper sense of social obligation can never escape this dual responsibility—to their own business firms and, as enlightened members thereof, to society—for business institutions are the major repositories of modern society's economic power.

Executives are expected to assert their leadership through these institutions. In the major segment of almost every community, private business firms and their executive representatives provide the opportunities for employment and the means of livelihood. They absorb a significant measure of society's best brainpower.

It is imperative that business leaders be both ingenious and efficient—that they be "creative" in finding *new* and *better* solutions, "productive" in intensive application of *currently available* solutions to the economic and technological problems of the private business firm. Public as well as private sectors of our economy have tremendous stakes in their acceptance of this responsibility.

For, should these indispensable entrepreneurs of modern society for some reason fail to take up this double obligation, disaster ensues. Commerce stagnates. Unemployment and poverty spread like the plague. The community's industrial capital quickly falls into disrepair. Locally organized agencies of benevolence dry up. The civilizing influence of a sensitive regard for others' rights and assorted miseries soon hardens into calloused indifference. Educational progress falters. The practice and the cultivated enjoyment of the arts wither away.

It is obvious, then, that the development of capable and socially perceptive recruits who can be trusted with this responsibility is always the problem above all problems of successful businesses everywhere.

Critical Dependence upon Executive Leadership

Modern society's critics, from the bilious commentaries of Thorstein Veblen a generation ago to the broad comedy of Abe Burrows and his co-authors in *How to Succeed in Business Without Really Trying,* have often been merciless in portraying the peculiar foibles of what they like to call the "organization man." They deplore the "depersonalizing" influence of modern commercial and industrial organizations. They insist that these tend inevitably to subordinate "individual virtues" like the courage of one's convictions, intellectual honesty, and creativity to less attractive "group virtues" such as adaptability to the crowd, eagerness to please, and passion for conformity.[1] But whatever validity these diverting pastimes may have, and very likely they have some, the supposedly warped victim is definitely not the ideal or sought-after type of business executive. Neither are the traits of character assumed to be uppermost in his nature by any means confined to business organizations.

The obvious prevalence of "organization men" in all ages and in all institutional settings actually should not be too much deplored. That most individuals have always responded to group

[1] The widely accepted image of the business leader, frequently drawn in not very flattering colors, is probably to be credited to modern writers of popular fiction. Professor Bernard Sarachek has written an interesting review of this influence in his short article, "The Image of the Corporate Executive in Recent Fiction," *Business and Society,* Vol. 5, No. 2 (1965), Roosevelt University, Chicago, Illinois.

pressures in this way—far from being tragic—has instead been a stabilizing influence. Organizations require followers as well as leaders. Willing followers provide the soothing sense of harmony in cooperative group effort. Courageous leaders are necessary to insure progress. The one is by definition dependent upon the other.

The truly basic problem of modern society, the problem of all organizations involving large numbers of people, is one of selecting and encouraging potential leaders, of providing opportunity to those who will know how to use it. Precisely, it is one of preserving the creative powers of individuals to their fullest extent without jeopardizing the continual need for compromise that is inherent in cooperative effort.

This need is not specific; it is general. It is not peculiar to the business firm; it pervades all organizational experience.

Purposive group action always results quite quickly in some perceptible stratification within the group. Recognizable leaders thus are set apart from those resigned to be led. Anthropologists tell us that even the most incoherent societies have their head men. This is the beginning of organization. Leadership, to be effective, must reconcile human differences and mediate between the participating individuals that constitute the rank and file and the necessarily restrictive goals set for joint accomplishment. Personal ferments must be brought under control so that an approximate condition of equilibrium may prevail.

Observance of established codes is essential. Both leaders and followers must take care to avoid tedious and senseless friction. But rigid conformity in patterns of thought is the thing most to be avoided.

A respected business executive of exceptionally broad experience has put the case substantially as follows:

> The organization process through which common men perform uncommon deeds cannot endure in the face of anything that deprives individuals of dignity, of belief in their own importance, of opportunity to test their powers of initiative, of experiencing the heartwarming spark of achievement.

> The highest possible premium must be placed on fresh and original ideas untrammeled by traditional thinking. On this there must be no inhibiting restrictions. Organizations exist and prosper only by giv-

ing free rein to men's minds and spirits in a climate of achievement moderated by the practice of good manners. Both of these environmental conditions must somehow be preserved, but there is a stout and significant difference between observance of simple amenities and coercion or subservience; between conformity with codes of behavior designed to facilitate social intercourse and individual surrender to uniformity of thought.[2]

When individual initiative shrivels and dies under the influence of sterile leadership, as this commentator concludes, "organizations cease to be organizations."

Executive Leadership an Individual Responsibility

The ultimate responsibility for vital and sensitive leadership in any organization is necessarily centered in the office of the chief executive. The deliberative responsibilities of management, whether legislative or judicial in nature, are essentially group activities. Executive directives aimed at producing action by those under authority are instead intensely personal. One man—not a group—must have final responsibility for decisions to which subordinates are expected to respond willingly. It is this supreme source of formal authority in the organization which is most likely to determine the pattern of executive leadership which comes to prevail in all the centers of decision making up and down the line of command.

Experience unmistakably endorses a monocratic structuring of executive authority at this particular level in the managerial hierarchy. If authority to decide a given critical issue is shared by several associates with equal mandates, sooner or later grave risk of strain and frustration always seems to develop. Government by commission or committee, if either sort of group, as such, really occupies the seat of executive authority, never quite succeeds in turning in a record of hardhitting and uncompromising performance.

The reason for this is that possession of positive authority is

[2] Paraphrased from an address by C. H. Greenewalt, then President, E. I. du Pont de Nemours, Inc., entitled "Individuals and Organizations," at Princeton University, 1961.

only one side of the shield of command. Authority, responsibility, and accountability must, by nature, be coextensive and inseparable in an ordered group existence. Authority imposes upon those to whom it is properly assigned the necessity of making decisions and directing actions impersonally and objectively for the organization. Responsibility implies personal accountability for the results which flow from these decisions and actions. Should the results fall short of expectations, there must be no occasion for uncertainty as to who is accountable, no opportunity to shift blame to others on the pretext that they too participated in the ill-fated decision, no time for equivocation and buck passing.

If the possessor of formal authority, of whatever kind, always receives it by an act of delegation from some higher source, the recipient, for order to prevail, must at the same time be assigned responsibility for its proper exercise. It ordinarily is implied, furthermore, that unless expressly prohibited he may, in turn, at his own discretion delegate this authority in whole or in part to others with corresponding responsibility for anticipated results.

The invariable rule is that authority can be redelegated unless it is restricted, but that responsibility can never be cleanly reassigned in the sense that the assigner is thereby absolved of accountability. The source from which he first derived his authority must still look to him for results.

When persistent shortcomings occur, no one in authority can be allowed to clear himself by insisting that his subordinates failed him or misrepresented what actually happened, or that he was not aware that things had gone wrong. It is precisely his business to see that his subordinates are dependable, that he is not deluded by misrepresentations, and that an adequate system of communication is established by which he is kept informed concerning his people's performance.

These are requirements that no executive can be allowed to waive on the pretext that the operation is too large, too complex, or too demanding of his time and attention to grasp fully. They are basic to control. As Professor Paul E. Holden once observed, one of the most challenging problems with which management in large-scale enterprise is confronted is "to delegate responsibility and authority, freeing itself of unnecessary detail, yet retaining the means for assuring that results will be satisfactory." [3] Challenging indeed, yet not impossible of achievement unless it is conceded that the practical limits of efficient administration have already been exceeded by today's large and complex organizational arrangements.

A particularly baffling problem of managerial responsibility is that presented by illegal action on the part of a corporate executive—for example, violation of the antitrust laws. [4] Who precisely, under the circumstances, is the transgressor? The executive who joined directly in the collusion complained of? Or his boss, who may or may not have known of and condoned it? Or, for that matter, the chief executive himself, in whose office the ultimate responsibility for observing the law resides?

From a strictly legal point of view, the answer is simple. He who initiated and participated in the forbidden action, obviously, is guilty. He clearly cannot plead innocence on the grounds that he merely carried out the directives or what he believed to be the wishes of higher authority. The question of corporate rectitude, however, is a problem of ethics more than of legal liability. It also raises the very practical consideration whether the organization has become so large as to render those in ultimate authority incapable of policing the behavior of their own subordinates.

The chief executive can scarcely be blamed for isolated errors of subordinates who expressly disobey orders or corporate policy. But, when they persist in their transgressions over extended periods without curb or question, who is responsible? The most charitable conclusion is that an indispensable element in the internal communication network of the firm—the function of executive surveillance and systematic audit—has broken down and needs to be repaired.

---

[3] Holden, Paul E., Fish, Lounsbury S., and Smith, Hubert L., *Top-Management Organization and Control,* Stanford University Press, 1941, pp. 8–9.

[4] The sensational convictions of representatives of the electrical equipment industry in 1961, and the widespread public discussion which they stimulated, provide a case in point.

Executive Leadership Demands Delegation

The system of authority centered in the executive high command must, as a practical matter, invariably be converted almost at once, beneath this focal point, into a hierarchical or pyramidal structure corresponding to the intended plan of organization. This is why delegation is so important. Acts of leadership whereby executives work through people are in reality acts of delegation. Managing, which always involves leadership, is, as Professor Herbert A. Simon [5] has remarked, "decision making," and the important skills for an executive are "decision-making skills." And decisions respecting the roles of subordinates must properly include determining who is to be granted authority in a given set of circumstances, what kind of authority to delegate, and what limits to place upon its exercise.

Aptitude in making these special decisions implies leadership skill of a very high order, which is rarely found to perfection and is frequently the despair of those who try to develop it in subordinates. Its possession often seems to have only a slight connection with intellectual achievement; sometimes men with the brightest minds are poor delegators and, in consequence, deficient as leaders of men. In fact, the art of delegation, unless learned early in executive experience, is not likely to be acquired to the point of real proficiency at all.

This common occupational defect among those aspiring to executive leadership is quite puzzling because failure to delegate is frequently indicative not so much of executive vices as of misapplied executive virtues. It has been observed over and over again that few chronic failures to delegate authority are traceable to gross indolence, neglect, or ingrained irresponsibility. In these few cases, the evidences of executive unfitness are so obvious to everyone as to be remedied sooner or later directly at the source.

Instead, it is readily apparent that many in authority fail to delegate because of a strong feeling of exhilaration at being in the midst of things—a valuable personal attribute if one aspires

[5] Simon, Herbert A., *The New Science of Management Decision,* Harper & Brothers, 1960, p. 4.

to leadership. Yet the personal urge to make essential decisions under the influence of this exhilaration may prove so intoxicating that it is unbearable to stand in the wings and share the experience with subordinates presumably less competent.

Some top men develop so fine a sense of craftsmanship that they find it well-nigh unbelievable that anyone else could do as well. Even in so routine a matter as a business letter or an office memo, the copy produced by a subordinate can scarcely be allowed to pass uncriticized and unchanged.

Some are too impatient. They find it much easier to act themselves than to guide inexperienced hands in needed action, little recognizing that budding executives grow and gain confidence best when given the privilege of making mistakes.

Personal rationalizations showing why authority in one's possession cannot safely be delegated are distinctly habit-forming, affecting especially the old grown used to dictatorial power. Addicts in advanced stages are prone to mistrust everyone's judgment but their own and, when found in high places, are fatal to good organization, which is clearly dependent upon judicious distribution of executive authority throughout the managerial structure. Overcentralization at focal decision-making centers congests communication and delays the decision-making process. It encourages, as men grow old in service, the development of indispensability complexes. It discourages the young, especially the more intelligent and ambitious with first-rate executive potential, many of whom become restive and leave before attaining real executive status. If persisted in, it delays the development of a vigorous managerial succession and inevitably creates the insidious earmarks of structural decay.

Positive resistance to this unwarranted decay is essential if it is not to get out of hand. Gluttons for executive power soon build formidable barriers against those in a position to share in the decision-making process. Subordinates in turn, even when they feel personally competent to deal with the subject in hand, readily succumb to the lazy habit of appealing to their superior for every decision. A neophyte must be of a particularly hardy breed to risk his unsupported judgment only to be accused of insubordination or overruled for no apparent reason (it seems to him) but to put him in his place.

Thus each locus of executive power is subtly subjected to forces which both push and pull it toward the center of final authority. Unless these forces are repelled by others—deliberately maintained—which are of equal intensity, there can be no orderly distribution of power within the hierarchical structure of management.

Acts of Delegation Must Be Explicit

But why, when rational delegation of executive authority is the only practicable means of overcoming the devastating influence of overcentralized power, is it not more generally practiced? Why do otherwise intelligent executives hold on so tenaciously to the reins of authority within their own jurisdiction? Why, in large organizations, is it ordinarily so difficult to maintain the rational ideal of decentralized authority in a sensible context?

The very obvious reason already mentioned—that the delegation of authority never permits a manager to escape responsibility for results—is doubtless valid. Prudent executives are likely to be reluctant to trust subordinates under these somewhat equivocal conditions. But this hesitancy makes it even more probable that there is a second reason—traceable, as is so often the case in organizational deficiencies, to faulty communication: Acts of delegation, to be effective, must be explicit. There must be no occasion for confusion as to just what is intended on the part of either the man who gives or the man who receives the mandate.

The remedy is simple: Imprecise distributions of executive authority may readily be minimized by carefully prepared executive job descriptions.

Some managements, it is true, despite the logic of this formality profess positive opposition to it. They insist on believing that any gestures tending to formalize the delegation of authority, such as a system of executive titles, deliberately contrived symbols of executive status, or explicit definitions of executive job content, not only quickly become obsolete but tend to discourage initiative and stifle innovation. This fantasy of freewheeling executives, each following his own bent yet working in close harmony with his fellows toward common objectives, may indeed be approximated in a small organization of tightly knit participants. Informality in human relationships has its attractions provided it can be preserved. But, as organizations grow, this soon becomes sheer nonsense. Teamwork always requires that teammates work in some sort of harness.

Organization is squarely based upon a systematic and clearly understood division of labor. Not only must specialized participants always know what is expected of them in their own jobs, but they also must know precisely how these fit into the general plan. Without this knowledge, the priceless coordinating influence is soon completely lost. To permit executives to reach for power wherever their personal interests or opportunistic urges prompt them to do so—or to retire into a self-constructed shell when they are too timid or polite to resist aggressive onslaughts by more forceful fellow executives—is bound to end in trouble. It is no more tenable than it would be to turn a horde of workmen loose in a shoe factory under orders to make shoes without first working out some systematic assignment of individual tasks.

Formal descriptions are not intended to record a detailed, blow-by-blow listing of authorized duties and responsibilities for executives in action. They should instead give a clear exposition of the organizational relationships within which the executive in question is expected to work. They should provide a concise outline of the specific areas of authority allotted to him. The necessities of executive control require that there be no uncertainty in these matters

There are always definite areas where each executive is empowered to act on his own discretion. These need to be spelled out. It is imperative that they be clearly distinguished from other areas or circumstances in which the manager's decisions are subject to review and approval, and still further from those where his authority is confined to recommendations and advice for the benefit of associates with whom the ultimate decision-making authority resides. Specific understanding on these matters need never hamper well-intentioned practitioners.

Old-fashioned executives sometimes profess irritation at restrictions of this sort. They frequently are the worst offenders in ignoring the ordinary amenities of command in intra-organizational contacts. They persist in neglecting the prescribed channels of authority and executive communication. They impetuously and gratuitously make decisions which others, whether subordinates or superiors, should make. They think nothing of discrediting subordinates in the eyes of their own subordinates by rudely giving or countermanding orders in open opposition to those already made.

These breaches of good manners in executive contacts are not evidences of strong leadership or of maturity in organization practice. They are decidedly frowned upon, for example, in military organizations—where without a doubt the delicate task of command is best understood and practiced. Possibly the correct view was never more concisely expressed than in the admonition that ''an order should not trespass upon the province of a subordinate. It should contain everything beyond the independent authority of the subordinate, but nothing more.'' [6]

Executive Leadership in a Free Society

Formal delegation of authority, it can readily be admitted, does not in a free society impose a very heavy obligation of unquestioning obedience upon those who from choice subject themselves to this authority. Acceptable credentials merely give the possessor the opportunity and the setting for creating and securing morale in the organization. The test of executives' success in establishing discipline and personal leadership lies in the degree to which they can develop and inspire among their subordinates loyalty to the system of executive authority.

The techniques of executive leadership likely to be effective in a truly free enterprise must be thoroughly attuned to these conditioning factors. Insubordinate employees may be dismissed. Quarrelsome stockholders may conceivably be bought out. Disgruntled customers can be told to seek service elsewhere. But these measures cannot be repeated over and over again without inviting chaos. Threatened reprisals are weak implements for

[6] U.S. Army Field Service Regulations.

disciplining troublesome employees, owners, or customers who have already in their own minds disassociated themselves from the cooperating group.

The private business executive's predicament in this respect is quite unique in the large-scale managerial and organizational experience of mankind. In other major institutional complexes —as, for example, in military or civil affairs backed by the full authority of an overriding state—the means of naked compulsion available to enforce executive authority are much in evidence. The contrast in managerial bargaining power is one which executives in private enterprise bent on preserving the health and survival of their firm are bound to be reminded of continually.

The comrade in a Communist state, for instance, even though he be a commissar, characteristically has little freedom of personal choice. He cannot withdraw when he becomes dissatisfied with his lot, simply because there is nowhere else for him to go. The soldier, forced against his will into military service, has no recourse but to submit to authority and surrender his accustomed freedom. And, even in matters of conscience, both clergy and church members often experience great travail of soul if they try to assert their independence of the mystical ties that bind them to organized ecclesiastical authority.

But in private business enterprise the intention is that the relations between leaders and followers should be as devoid of formal compulsion as can be contrived. No clumsy show of executive authority will ever put matters right in this environment when things really get out of hand. The independence derived from voluntary association requires of those who would manage a fine artistry in human relations. To succeed, executives must rely upon positive, not negative, motivation. They must persuade rather than coerce. They must learn how to inspire morale. Fear of punishment, should constituted authority be flaunted, is not an effective deterrent to free men.

Much as executives, at their wits' end to restore order, may wish for coercive power, if they are wise they will stoutly defend their subordinates' right of dissent and power to make this right effective by voluntary withdrawal. More than 25 years ago, Chester I. Barnard helped to give organizational thinking a new and constructive turn in this direction. This unusual business executive with a philosophical turn of mind and a noteworthy faculty for lucid exposition declared that "the decision as to whether an order has authority or not rests with the persons to whom it is addressed and does not reside in 'persons of authority' or those who issue these orders." In other words, no authority can be made effective if those under submission do not enable it to be. Ultimate authority "rests upon the acceptance or consent of individuals"—that is, those to whom it applies.[7]

The liberating nature of free institutions built squarely on voluntary association lends broad validity to this view. Where cooperation is truly voluntary, the web of executive authority must be thoroughly imbued with the concept of stewardship, of service, of proffered opportunity for growth, of promised satisfaction to those who join the group. Without these, it is unlikely to be supported by willing participation.

Formal and Informal Executive Authority

Actually, between formal authority—that is, *authority of position*—and informal authority, sometimes designated as *authority of leadership,* there need be no real conflict. They are, in fact, inseparable in practice. Authority of position, so called, seldom bestows automatically upon its possessor authority of leadership. Nor can authority of leadership ever be wholly perfected without some sustaining sanction of authority of position.

It is significant that in the three broad areas of human endeavor in which organizational experience has reached the highest levels of maturity—the church, the state, and the military—great care is invariably lavished upon establishing *authority of position,* beyond cavil, for all those occupying seats of power. Elaborate attention is given in all these particular institutional complexes to keeping bright the symbols of authority. Punctilious deference to rank and careful observance of rituals and ordination proceedings are no mere concessions to

[7] Barnard, Chester I., *The Functions of the Executive,* Harvard University Press, 1938. See Chapter XII, on "The Theory of Authority."

human vanity or outgrown traditions of pomp and circumstance. Individuals may or may not prove wholly worthy of their trust. So be it. The office itself is made a special object of veneration. Failure of the incumbent to fulfill the ideals of leadership completely, should it occur, is certain to prove less disastrous when he moves in this aura of respect and dignity.

In all forms of compulsory association and in military organizations in particular, this special deference to authority of position is clearly justified. But without the essential element of personal leadership the evidences of rank are truly pretentious "brass" even here.

Personal "styles" of leadership—doubtless dependent more upon the man than upon the nature of his job—seem to be, in fact, as diverse as the personalities of the leaders themselves. Among military leaders, for example (even those few clearly set apart as though predestined for special hero worship), the innate qualities which have made for particular effectiveness apparently follow no set pattern. In some—Generals Lee and MacArthur, to cite only two—the mark of destiny was unmistakable; evidences of developing genius were clearly discernible quite early in their careers. Commanding presence, self-assurance in manner, superb intellectual and emotional endowments, firmly imbedded moral convictions, illustrious family heritage —what else could be added in evidence of potential leadership? Their rapid promotion in rank was merely confirmation of the obvious.

But sometimes men who appear to be exceptions to the general rule best illustrate the qualities which distinguish leaders of men. For a person like General Grant, for instance—undistinguished in presence, unassuming in manner, unexceptional in youth, and apparently uncertain of his purpose even with approaching maturity—the paths of glory would seem at the outset to have been strangely barren and forbidding. Who would have marked him for leadership?

No one ever started his military career under less propitious circumstances: Dogged by petty misfortunes, temptations, and loneliness, he was maligned by suspicious civilians; subjected to slanderous treatment by the press; mistrusted and humiliated in the field by superiors less competent, less aware of the hard road ahead, less courageous and resourceful than he. Fortunately, his deep perception of the strengths and weaknesses of the raw recruits in his charge (born and reared, as was he himself, in the crude communities of the Middle West) won from his troops the confidence which was denied him by his superiors in rank. His quiet assurance and indomitable will, his stubborn faith in the ultimate outcome of the cause for which they fought gave this singularly self-effacing man a quality of leadership rarely surpassed. When the time for testing came, he led his hardening troops relentlessly on to victory.

Authority of position usually is the forerunner which provides the opportunity to develop authority of leadership. In men less dedicated, it is almost indispensable to that end. But in Grant's case the order of precedence seems to have been in the main reversed. Hard-won authority of leadership eventually gained recognition from his Commander in Chief and brought him supreme authority of position as General of the Armies of the North.

In comparison, of course, the voluntary associations of business place less emphasis upon the ritualistic observance of authority. Most businessmen would be distinctly self-conscious and impatient if compelled to pay attention to the insignia of rank and the stilted etiquette of formal communication between officers and men. These formalities which seem so important in military affairs—and, it may be, properly so—would in the free and easy relations of business executives seem sheer vanity and downright foolishness.

Different places, naturally, give rise to different customs. Indeed, it is ordinarily assumed, with cause, that there must be some systematic scale of executive titles representing progressive levels in the managerial hierarchy. Some form of dignified internal communication respecting an executive appointment helps to get the appointee off to a good start. Some formal statement of the duties and responsibilities of the various members helps to establish a better working executive team. Some attention to office appointments in keeping with the respective ranks of the tenants helps to establish executive self-esteem (and the status of subordinates). Anyone who has ever had the task of designing an executive suite knows full well that these ways of expressing executive dignity are by no means taken lightly.

The trappings of office are not idle formalities which may be neglected with impunity. A business organization, like any complicated structure, must be systematically planned, designed in detail, and documented by specifications and working rules before its form and substance can be understood by those destined to function within it. What might be termed the outward symbols of authority are essential components in the system of internal communication whereby a sound basis of executive influence is provided. Authority of position is thus assured. Whether men who possess it also achieve authority of leadership depends upon their own efforts and resources.

Both personal prestige and outward symbols are indispensable if order is to prevail. A vice president would be foolish to think that merely because he *is* a vice president his authority will be respected. But this official recognition, nevertheless, provides a base upon which his own behavior can create the essential conditions of respect and properly directed action.

There is a magic in executive titles and status which everyone in authority would do well to learn how to use. What organization man does not understand the chain of feverish activity almost certain to be put in motion when word is passed down that "the chief wants it," "the president is thinking thus-and-so," or "the boss is wondering if it could be done this way"![8] The channel through which this message flows may be a chief clerk or staff assistant of no great status, but the voice is that of the chief executive. Everyone within hearing springs into action to prove that he is in tune.

The Conditions of Assent

If, in the final analysis, the effective authority enjoyed by any executive is explicitly determined by the willingness of his sub-

---

[8] The issuance of directives in tentative form and by indirection, sometimes described as "sending up a trial balloon," occasionally has its uses as a means of conserving executive authority. It protects the executive office from suspicion of fallability should things go wrong; it stimulates subordinates to exercise initi-

ordinates to accept it, how can he make sure of earning this necessary endorsement?

There are criteria by which the acceptability of executive orders can within reasonable limits be predetermined. Civilized men, fortunately, have an instinctive respect for order and authority. When freely joined for a common purpose, they naturally have no deliberate disposition to defeat this purpose insofar as they understand it.

In every association of persons, executive orders, with some exceptions, fall within what has aptly been called "the broad zone of indifference." Within this zone men of goodwill freely give their consent because they are neutral about the outcome, believe implicitly in the reliability of their leader, or positively support the intended aim. It is the exceptions that cause concern and require that executives, to be successful, thoroughly understand the conditions of consent—the terms on which their orders are likely to be obeyed.

There are three main conditions of consent which executives must keep in mind:

1. *Executive orders are not likely to be obeyed unless believed by those to whom they are addressed to be consistent with the purposes of the organization as these are understood.* The Allied Military Commander of 1918, Marshall Foch, once declared: "There can be no collective harmony in the active sense in any organization unless each and every one concerned knows what the purpose is." These words from so renowned a military commander a half-century ago have a strangely modern ring. They would scarcely have been understood in an earlier generation by the men of "The Light Brigade" whose famous charge the poet memorialized as a glorious episode in the history of battles. This was indeed a superb example of how men can discipline themselves to accept the prospect of sudden death. But to candid modern minds it was also a stupid sacrifice of brave men, devoid of even the most elementary requirements of a calculated risk.

Free men from the highest to the lowest are disposed to test

ative in taking action; and it encourages willing collaboration by permitting those of lesser authority to share in the credit due when things turn out as planned.

the orders of superiors by this standard of consistency with purpose. Employees who are conditioned to high standards of workmanship and who take pride in a shop tradition of quality production will quickly feel a sense of outrage when ordered to slight their work, just as they will protest that they are being asked to do the impossible when their orders call suddenly for tightening the standards of workmanship. In either case, the new orders seem inconsistent with the purposes of the operation as they understand them. What is required as a corrective is not so much instruction as explanation of why the new method of operation has become important.

2. *There must be agreement that whatever is expected does not encroach upon the generally accepted personal prerogatives of those giving consent.* Men habitually draw a reasonably sharp line between demands which by custom fall within what they concede to be reasonable conditions of employment and those which seem excessive. If job requirements are to be changed, they must be carefully explained; else resentment is almost sure to follow. Even when the change is clearly in the workmen's own interest, suitable preparation is essential if it represents a sudden break with past practice and discipline. Safety precautions, for example, are notoriously resented and disregarded unless properly presented.

3. *Executive authority, if it is to be willingly obeyed, must be generally recognized by those who give consent as consistent with the limits of formal authority prescribed for their superior officer.* To exceed one's authority, if it be generally known, is to run grave risk of encountering hostility and grudging obedience. Those expected to obey are quick to disapprove infringements of standards to which they themselves are expected to conform. Unless the deviation is clearly justified by the good of the organization as subordinates understand it, there is bound to be resentment.

*   *   *

The capacity for leadership by which executives make their authority effective is an intensely personal thing. It is not dependent solely upon delegations from above, though proper credentials are expected. It is dependent upon the attitude and conviction of the leader as mirrored in the acceptance of his followers.

The rules for acceptance are quite positive. They are based upon mutual confidence; upon respect for one's superiors and, in turn, for one's subordinates; upon unswerving loyalty to the system of authority which has been established. Good leaders must first be good followers. For, to give orders with assurance that they will be unquestioningly obeyed, one must be prepared to take orders ungrudgingly as well. The executive who is critical of his superiors, attributing to them real or imagined slights and errors in judgment, ought first to make doubly sure that he is not seeing in them his own shortcomings as viewed by his subordinates.

III

Executive Functions: Direction

PRIVATE CORPORATIONS, WHICH ARE THE INTEGRAL PARTS OF THE FREE
enterprise system, set the general patterns of executive behavior. As interacting members of this system—some large, many
small yet able to survive by their own resourcefulness—they
compete for business. Judged by the criterion of customer service, the system of which they are a part is wonderfully effective.
Free and competitive markets are clearly superior in achieving
this essential service goal to the maneuverings of some auto-
cratic but considerably less than omniscient central planning
agency in a corporate state.

As we have already observed, it is a great convenience to attribute to these corporate entities, as legal creations, the characteristics of persons. To fulfill the requirements of this useful
fiction, corporations must, like all persons, possess certain
identifiable traits. They must have the intelligence to make rational decisions and the determination to take appropriate actions. They must communicate, be capable of creating and
projecting a distinctive personal image recognizable by all those
with whom interchanges must be maintained. They must display
some reasonably precise and acceptable scale of values, be
guided by some socially approved moral code.

Desirable personality traits such as these, if they are to be
identified as qualities of the corporate complex, must be supplied by executives working within prescribed jurisdictional lim-

its. The indispensable functions include *direction, representation,* and *evaluation.* Taken together, these are in effect the three legs of the managerial stool, giving stability to executive performance. Slight any one and the system of executive authority begins to totter and disintegrate. Deficiencies soon are reflected in an enterprise lacking in purpose, lacking in color, and lacking in the discipline that is so essential to maintaining position in the competitive struggle.

Scope of the Executive's Directive Function

The directive function of management nearly always occupies the forefront of executive attention. He who would grasp the corporate reins and assume executive burdens must above all else possess the capacity for analytical thinking and decisive action. He must initiate plans and make sure of their fulfillment. He must make decisions and must, in turn, allow decisions to be made. He must clothe these decisions in the sense of urgency which stimulates others to action with a positive sense of direction.

In exercising these responsibilities, executives need always an instinct for accurate timing. They are depended upon to develop within the corporate framework a pervasive sense of coordinated purpose, guiding and inspiring the collective group of specialists comprising the firm. Above all, they are expected to act rationally, thinking and deciding in the firm's best interests with wisdom and assurance.

This prime executive function involves—

- Establishing tenable goals.
- Developing operating programs consistent with these goals.
- Initiating appropriate and timely action.
- Setting up a coordinated system of carry-through so as to encourage and guarantee positive results of the quality desired.

To master this foremost task of management requires acute awareness of all pertinent data bearing upon relevant decisions and the prescience to grasp their probable effects upon circumstances, things, and persons.

Attendant decisions and actions, to be sure, are always subject to restraints, for, as in all social endeavors, business executives are never entirely free agents. Tradition and precedent quite properly influence them continually in some measure. The past and the future are closely joined in every institution. In some, as in the church and only less so in the state, veneration of this heritage from generations long since past is a powerful disciplining influence upon those currently in authority. In others, and particularly in business enterprise, the influence of the past may be less in evidence, though who would say that even here tradition and precedent are totally irrelevant to executive thinking and actions? Each new day is one more link between an irrevocable past and a future which still can be molded.[1]

It clearly is essential for all in power at any given time, in business as elsewhere, to be attentive to the insistent promptings of past experience. These give a reassuring sense of perspective. They discourage opportunism in executive decisions. Executive wisdom always depends both upon lively appreciation of what the experience of the past teaches and upon understanding of today's needs.

Responsible men in business as in politics are never contemptuous of tradition and precedent. They refuse to be enslaved by the past, but they recognize in it valid bench marks setting the course for a flexible policy adapted to the demands of a changing present. True liberals, no less than cautious conservatives though with different emphasis, recognize the essential interrelatedness of past, present, and anticipated future which incautious extremists of either left or right choose stubbornly to ignore.

The unique distinction of private enterprise which those who exercise the directive function must never for one moment forget is that its goals are necessarily customer-oriented. Seek-

[1] Drawn from a convocation address, "The Expansion of Economic Opportunity," by Arthur F. Burns at the University of Chicago in September 1960.

ing out, influencing, serving, and retaining customer acceptance is the only way survival can be guaranteed. All efforts, programs, and supplementary goals must be centered around this primary goal.

There are other goals, to be sure: profits, of course, and the creation of a good place to work, among others. The quest for profits is an unremitting executive occupation. The need to create and preserve loyalty and efficiency in the workforce likewise is ever insistent. But while profits are properly the primary concern of owners and creditors, just as a good place to work is an absorbing goal of employees, managers with direct responsibility for keeping alive the spark of enterprise must look first to market acceptability. Without this, there cannot for long be either profits or a contented workforce.

Executive plans, budgets, production and delivery schedules, cost estimates, and income expectations thus must always be predicated upon what the market holds in store. What products and services should one try to sell? Who can be induced to buy? Where can potential customers be found? What is necessary to fan latent interest into actual orders? How can competition be met without disastrous erosion of profit margins? These are key questions in every successful business program. They call always for a deliberate sense of direction, but they cannot concern the president's office alone. They must in actual fact penetrate the very core of the organization.

Customers are not irresistibly drawn to the place of business where there is no deeply ingrained conviction that "the customer is always right." Profits rarely are satisfactory in the concern where few are profit-conscious. The thing that makes a good place to work is the concerted effort of everyone to make it so. Individual members must be competent and efficient, but added to their competence and efficiency must always be the group factor of the effectiveness with which they work together.

The Necessity for Coordinated Action

Teamwork is not achieved simply through the cooperative efforts of the individual players. There must be a guiding mind observing and acting above the level of personal struggle in the game itself. This vantage point permits sufficiently objective detachment to curb the personal ambitions and relieve the emotional tensions of the players. Instead, the interests of the team are put in proper perspective. Members of an orchestra, no matter how sensitive and technically proficient, can never reproduce the symphonic vision of the composer without the disciplining guidance of the conductor.

This miracle of coordination, whether on the playing field, in the concert hall, or within the confines of the business firm—this "act of regulating diverse elements so as to give harmonious results"—is the highest achievement of leadership. It is the very essence of this function of direction.

The indispensable requirements of coordination in business operations differ with circumstances. There are, for example, *time* coordination and *place* coordination. Realization of these requires that actions and things intended as identical be so regulated that they are identical regardless of accident of time or place of performance. The great engineering principle of interchangeable parts on which modern production is based depends upon this identicalness.

Sequential coordination, to cite another example, implies that interrelated actions are to be performed precisely in the sequence most conducive to the desired end. Proper planning and scheduling of operations are the means of achieving this objective.

Or it may be necessary to fashion things or perform actions representing essential parts of a whole in a manner which insures that they will fit together exactly as intended. When applied to persons, this *organic* coordination (the "coordination of specialists") is the essential condition in all justifiable division of labor, the very foundation of technological efficiency.

The necessity for organic coordination manifestly permeates all phases of operating a business. If carefully conceived and planned, with every anticipated turn of fortune provided for in advance, the program, whatever it may be, can scarcely fail. Otherwise there is only the slimmest of chances that it will succeed.

Take, for instance, a common business problem—that of introducing a new product. Almost everyone in the organization is immediately involved. The market must be estimated. The product itself must be tested. Financial requirements must be determined. A promotional program must be adopted. Salesmen must be specially trained. Manufacturing and procurement arrangements must be matured. Packaging, inventory requirements, shipping, warehousing, delivery schedules, budgets, and a host of other considerations must be taken into account and appropriate activity set in motion at the proper time. Neglect any of these, provide for them without due consideration of their essential interrelatedness—and the whole program begins to falter for lack of coordination.

This all-pervasive process of establishing system is the strategic ingredient in the function of direction.

The Tools of Executive Direction

A specific act of direction always originates in an idea conceived by some executive and developed through his subsequent decisions. If the idea is novel or of great moment, the decision which sets the activity in motion must necessarily be made by someone in high authority. Executives at lower levels in management will scarcely dare or be permitted to take the risk of misjudgment. In time, the activity will become repetitive. That is, the precedent of the first decision will inevitably be remembered, the lower-level executives (in whose jurisdiction the need for the decision very likely first became apparent) will be reassured by it, and eventually they will themselves make the necessary decision without reference to higher authority.

It is in this manner that business *policies* usually are born. A policy is "the principle or rule of action to be applied in deciding or dealing with a given set of circumstances or actions." It can be, and sometimes is, worked out in elaborate detail in anticipation of future requirements for executive action. More often, it develops out of the natural process of following precedent. But, no matter how policies originate, they become—once established—the cement of consistency which binds authoritative decisions and actions into a coordinated whole.

Policies lend a sense of assurance to subordinates and a sense of authorizing validity to executive actions. Policies save the labor of repetitive decisions at higher levels of management. As soon as one has obtained currency in given circumstances, its routine application can take place without appealing again to the level of management which first stated it.

Policies crystallize executive thinking and action. They encourage managerial team play without discouraging individual initiative. They provide the guideposts in all group endeavor. They set the general pattern but leave room for local adaptation to exceptions. Policies, in short, make possible the realization of that all-pervasive goal of orderly executive behavior—*to decentralize authority and still retain centralized control.*

Business organizations justify their existence, of course, not by the policies they profess—important as these are—but by the goods or services they produce. Broadening markets with common requirements quickly make possible a substantial degree of similarity in these products or services. This quest for uniformity promotes efficiency in operations provided the model chosen for emulation is correct.

The result is *standardization.* It is an essential ingredient in modern technology, though actually it is of fairly recent origin. Its application in industry has roughly paralleled the development of modern engineering science. It has made mass production possible.

Standards, defined as "preconceived types or models with which subsequently contrived units or things are expected to conform," make possible design uniformity in point of time and place. Just as policies secure the coordination of ideas, standards secure the coordination of things and methods.

Standards establish, in advance, essential interrelations as well as differences in product components. They provide assurance that intended product goals can be achieved. Like policies, they are executive labor-saving devices. They make unnecessary the continual preoccupation, by executives up and down the line of command, with the details of repetitive operations. These can be relegated almost to the lowest level of supervision simply because they are repetitive and therefore become routine.

Standards provide a norm for judging current performance. They assist in the evaluating process.

Standards make it possible to think through the details of an operation at the drawing board, where engineering changes can be quickly and cheaply made. They facilitate communication. A coordinated program embodying essential specifications which will govern engineering, manufacturing, and sales activities can thus be set up before actual work in the shop or sales office is begun.

Standardized *things* make possible standardized *methods*. Provided the operation is to be repeated a sufficient number of times, much thought and effort can be profitably spent in working out "the best design" and "the best method." The goal of maximum efficiency is by this means brought nearer to realization.

Production engineers, in other words, continually put into practice what economists have often perceived: that the process of standardization and particularly the search for *good* standards are not much subject to the law of diminishing returns. Given an operation sufficiently repetitive—which is characteristically the case in modern manufacture—almost any amount of expense can be justified in perfecting even minute detail in either standard designs or standard methods. Infinitesimal reductions in unit cost and slight improvements in product adaptability are magnified in mass production.

Where division of labor is the rule, repetitive operations emphasize the role of still another set of tools in achieving coordination. *Procedures* become important. The process involved in achieving some important end result (such as launching a new product) usually cuts across numerous departmental boundaries in confusing detail. A predetermined order of attack is necessary to avoid general turmoil. The sequence of events must be charted; the responsibilities of each participant must be carefully spelled out; paperwork must be designed to avoid duplication. Each step must be scheduled with precision, or else there is grave danger that the whole process will be caught in a bureaucratic quagmire. Procedures, properly streamlined, provide guidance through this confusion.

Policies, standards, and procedures thus represent the means by which purposeful system is developed in an organization. All three introduce order where otherwise chaos and frustration would occur. Through them executives, sure of the road they have determined to pursue, communicate this assurance to those who follow.

There is an old saying, handed down from manual craftsmanship days, that "a good workman never quarrels with his tools." Just so, no alert executive in the performance of his directive function ever minimizes the importance of policies, standards, or procedures. These represent the basic tools of his craft. To create and use them effectively requires, first of all, calm, deliberative thinking and, second, forthright, unequivocal decisions, promptly implemented by energetic action.

The Process of Executive Decision

The mechanics employed in fulfilling these two requirements are quite different. Fixing accountability for decisions initiating action, as we have seen, is greatly facilitated if responsibility for those decisions can readily be identified with specific individuals. But the deliberative processes which necessarily precede decision and action are essentially group activities, always dependent, in turn, upon good internal communication. It is these deliberative processes which must be relied upon to explain personal attitudes, expose individual prejudices, and air divergent but honestly maintained points of view, freely and naturally, among the members of the group.

The committee is the major formal device which in every organization supplements the informal communication that occurs continually between all articulate human beings with a mutuality of interest. The real utility of committees is, however, an issue on which executive opinions and inclinations differ sharply. In some organizations, they are used upon almost every occasion. A large proportion of executive time may indeed be consumed in committee meetings—to the point where the entire decision-making process is reduced to a formalized committee type of management. At the other extreme in executive practice, as a competent observer has remarked, "the committee has perhaps come in for more ribbing—and serious criticism—than any other management technique." [2]

The major purpose in setting up a committee is obviously economy of executive time and effort—by encouraging collaboration among staff executives in a joint attack upon complicated managerial problems and between line and staff in communicating recommendations by the latter and the action subsequently decided upon by the former. Failure to restrict the use of this device is without doubt the reason why committees, even when properly organized and controlled, often achieve only disappointing results.

Weak line executives who shun their responsibility for decisions usually lean heavily upon committees. They justify this course by a professed desire to "coordinate" group opinion by attempted reconciliation of the proposed decision, in advance, with the thinking of everyone who might possibly object to it. But the resulting consensus, when it is finally determined, frequently comes too late to be useful! The occasion for achieving unanimity has been passed by because action could not wait. When decisions and actions are critical, any action is often better than no action.

The final decision-making phase of the executive function of direction is, in fact, rarely if ever a legitimate responsibility of a committee. Group participation in. the necessary investigating and fact gathering which should precede every executive decision to the extent that time permits is indispensable, but this is something quite different from group decision making. One executive, certainly in the best of positions to observe committees in action, has asserted that committees are of value only for exchanging ideas. It is individuals who must always make the decisions and take responsibility for their consequences.[3] Within these guidelines and subject to these limitations, committees supplement and aid executives in giving the organization the needed sense of direction; but, when the exchange of ideas

[2] Lohmann, M. R., Dean of the College of Engineering, Oklahoma State University, *Top Management Committees*, AMA Research Study 48, 1961, p. 8.

[3] Based on a statement by Robert S. McNamara, U.S. Secretary of Defense, in *Armed Forces Management*, November 1961.

has served its purpose, each executive in his appointed sphere must make the decision and mobilize the appropriate action.

Activities in particular need of coordination throughout the structure of management always must, for precision's sake, be brought into association as directly as possible through a common superior authority. Focal points at which decision-making responsibilities converge are to be found at all levels in the structure, and they must be manned by executives courageous enough to make their own decisions and capable of seeing that their subordinates act accordingly—in harmony rather than as rivals. Committees may have the best intentions in the world; but, without the electrifying sort of leadership which can bring an end to debate when everyone has had his say, their deliberations are likely to result in conversation instead of decision.

The irrationality of divided authority in the decision-making aspect of the directive function has always impressed dynamic business executives. Probably they would almost universally approve the view expressed by one of them in the quotation which follows:

> To check with [other opinions] after arriving at one's own decision tentatively is the most obvious sort of prudence, but to check as a substitute for [one's own] thinking is not the stuff of which leadership is made. . . .
>
> Our success . . . depends upon decisiveness, and that is a function of individual judgment. Committees breed indecision, and divided authority stagnation. When all the conferences have been held, and all the viewpoints have been heard, there comes a time at every level of management when one man must decide. . . . He must bring it about that others will carry out his decisions with understanding and enthusiasm. He must lead and not command.[4]

And the team he is required to lead must be one that he himself would choose.

[4] Randall, Clarence B., *A Creed for Free Enterprise*, 1952, pp. 164, 46, 47. Copyright 1952 by Clarence B. Randall. Reprinted by permission of Atlantic— Little, Brown and Co., publishers.

IV

Executive Functions: Representation

THE SECOND BASIC RESPONSIBILITY WHICH EXECUTIVES MUST ASSUME within the corporate structure is to serve as corporate spokesmen. This task constitutes the function of representation.

To act in this capacity requires a talent for lucid communication and calculated behavior. If the corporate entity is to be accepted as a respected member of the community, it must observe the neighborly refinements of good citizenship. If it is to be taken seriously in the commitments attendant upon ordinary business transactions, its spokesmen must create a reputation for dependability. If the corporate personality is to be both recognizable and admirable, management must be capable of resolving inner conflicts of interest and speaking with one voice.

It is inherent in institutions that these conflicts should exist. In every business enterprise, there are always latent or active misunderstandings involving owners, executive associates, the workforce, suppliers, customers, the community, competitors.

To succeed in relieving potential tensions, executives must possess a deep understanding of the motives which prompt men to take the rational or irrational stands they do. Executives must be articulate in transmitting communications, sensitive in receiving them, capable of making plain the basic needs of the enterprise they represent. Failure either externally or internally will eventually destroy the foundation on which the very existence of cooperative effort depends.

Executives must have clarity of vision, the patience and ingenuity to seek out a basis for compromise when compromise is essential, and the stubborn will to stand firm when the enduring good of the enterprise calls for a halt to making further concessions. Many of the modern executive's most insistent internal problems are doubtless traceable directly to his own lack of backbone, his unwillingness to stand up and be counted when essential prerogatives of management are being contested.

The "corporate image"—to borrow a threadbare but expressive figure of speech from the art of public relations—is distinctly a thing of value. Institutions as well as individuals are judged by the impressions they create. The basic unit in business, the corporate entity or firm, is composed of persons each of whom harbors his own private ambitions, yet it is still expected to possess sufficient cohesion in goals to present a common front to outsiders. Responsibility for projecting the desired personalized image rests inevitably with management. It is an essential element in the executive's role. No one else is available for this task.

Stockholders, for instance, develop almost complete detachment respecting internal organizational matters. Employees, torn by conflicting sentiments and class rivalries, tend to place obligation to their corporate employer fairly low in their scale of personal loyalties. Customer attachments likewise grow insecure and buying habits fickle in markets abundantly supplied with desired goods and services. Creditors have only one real concern: that, no matter what happens, their own privileged position shall be respected. The community, grown accustomed to corporate acknowledgment of its neighborhood responsibilities, becomes more and more urgent in its demands, while the administrative pressures of government upon private business are continually more pervasive and persistent.

In all this clamor, there must be at least one voice sufficiently nonpartisan to speak out for the business. Someone must stoutly maintain against all contenders, within and without, its capacity to compete with spirit and vigor on equal terms in the marketplace. Our private economy, if it is to be healthy, requires this.

Scope of the Representation Function

The function of corporate representation has many facets. Executives must—

- Serve as official spokesmen in dealings with internal vested interests and with outsiders.
- Interpret institutional objectives.
- Negotiate contractual agreements.
- Protect the corporate reputation and defend corporate interests.
- Enforce disciplined internal observance of corporate commitments.

Under certain circumstances, executives must even accept personal accountability for corporate behavior. They must always operate with the haunting knowledge that they have no immunity from penalty for corporate misdeeds similar to that provided for owners.

A detached observer might conceivably conclude that this function of representation in the institutions of business, especially as it concerns their external relationships, is indifferently performed. It is doubtless the most underrated of management's multiple responsibilities. This stranger might reason further that, in modern society, business is not simply a means of livelihood but for vast numbers of people, directly or indirectly, an almost completely absorbing way of life. He might well wonder under the circumstances why the true nature, aims, and contributions of private business enterprise in relation to human well-being are not better understood, more highly valued, viewed with less suspicion.

The emphasis in this widespread uneasiness about the motives of private business, our observer would soon discover, concerns especially "big business." This is true despite the fact that quite possibly these suspect corporate members of the community, because they are continually exposed to the white light of public scrutiny, must for safety's sake follow the path of rectitude much more carefully than their smaller neighbors.

The integrity of "small business," though manifestly managed by men who are no more nor less honest than those who manage big business, does seem to be granted much more graciously. There are so many small businesses, and they tend to be identified for all of us with recognizable persons. We rarely fear or mistrust greatly the things or persons we are most familiar with.

The somber smoke screen of mistrust and misunderstanding which so often surrounds corporate affairs reflects in part a heritage which is permeated with past misdemeanors and unsocial conduct. Unquestionably, there are those who see in the subtle discrediting of business motives some profitable advantage to their own dubious ends. Stranger still, there are at times sincere observers of the American scene who claim to have discovered in the free enterprise system "no principle of social good." These unfriendly voices, no matter where they come from, make the processes of redemption extremely hard.

It is not that businessmen have blunter social instincts, less personal warmth and common charity than other men. No one could believe this who has witnessed at first hand the enormous personal effort quietly and humbly expended by business leaders in every urban community to promote essential social services and welfare.

It is not that they "protest too much." They certainly are no more than ordinarily open to the charge of insincerity. Indeed, when businessmen and their corporate trustworthiness are subjected to vicious attack, they appear in comparison with their critics peculiarly inept and hesitant in rising to their own defense. The habit of authority acquired in their executive experience makes them—or so it often seems—distinctly self-conscious in public controversy. Few executives appear to have much of the talent for persuasive debate which is elementary equipment for men who aspire to political or labor leadership.

Protecting the Company's Good Name

Good corporate as well as personal citizenship is, of course, more a matter of action than of profession, and the action begins at home in local community affairs. This is where executives must first pass the test of social approval.

There was a time when it was more or less expected that an industrial neighborhood should bear the unmistakable evidence of depressing blight for miles around. Men might grumble sullenly, but no one expected anyone to do much about it. To live in such surroundings was the price of employment opportunities. Prevention of air contamination or water pollution presented a technological problem which no one expected to be solved, certainly not by the corporate residents or their executives who created and permitted the public nuisance.

This callousness in public relations no longer is tenable. New factors in community life have awakened management: neighborhood pressures, a more civilized appreciation of esthetic values, techniques for correcting these sordid influences, and—not least—growing insistence by a labor force that fortunately is no more content to remain silent about an uninviting home environment than about subsistence levels of livelihood. Industry is gradually adopting new concepts of its public responsibilities.

It has become good business to be on the positive side of neighborhood improvement. Slum *prevention* is being found much less costly in corporate goodwill and tax assessments than slum *clearance* after the community damage is done.

The corporate image as reflected in good labor relations and wholesome working conditions, strict adherence to reliability and decency in contractual relations, and attentive consideration to customer sensibilities obviously ought to be the concern of everyone, whether employer or employee. A discourteous salesman, an inattentive receptionist, a clumsy waiter, or a reckless truck driver (as we all know from countless petty irritations) inevitably cancels out much painstaking work by his employer's public relations department. Heedless employee conduct damages the company's reputation in the eyes of those who are victimized, but an alienated public is more likely to blame management than the offending employee.

Hirelings frequently feel obligated to do no more than they have been told or taught to do. Basically, therefore, the training and the discipline essential to insure acceptable standards of employee conduct in public are the responsibility of management.

It is no miscarriage of justice that the public blames the employer, not the employee, for persistent breaches of good human relations. The habit of imitation is strong in human beings. A spirit of wholesome goodwill in public dealings, when consistently practiced by employees, is usually inspired by the pattern of personal warmth and instinctive good manners set by men placed high in the company hierarchy. Executives enjoying the broad authority of leadership invariably "cast long shadows."

Representing the Owners in Corporate Affairs

The representative function has internal as well as external aspects. The interests and conduct of proprietors must be reconciled with those of employees. And owners must, in turn, have a sympathetic understanding of employee sensibilities if reasonable harmony is to prevail.

To be sure, the rights of private property give owners a specially favored position in securing attentive representation by executives in the internal politics of the firm. Their official status is derived from this fact. But in practice this natural allegiance on the part of the executives may be more apparent than real.

The sheltered position and faltering voice of the individual corporate stockholder, if not his studied indifference to his inherent rights as such, have modified considerably the relationship between owner and manager. That which in a nonincorporated firm is an exact identity of interest or, at the very least, a close kinship between principal and personal agent quickly becomes, in the corporate structure, a purely impersonal relationship requiring conscious effort by executives to maintain a semblance of communication with total strangers.

Even executive preoccupation with profits is not so much an evidence of solicitous partisanship respecting owners as often is supposed. Profits in our economic scheme of things are indispensable as a source of capital for expansion of plant and facilities and, hence, future growth. Without these, both the firm and its management soon lose position. But, to management, profits also have a more personal meaning. Owners are interested because profits belong to them whereas, for managers, profits are the most concrete and convenient index of their own success or failure.

It is true that the executive's special obligation to ownership is beyond dispute. In the annual report and in stockholders' meetings, executives acknowledge this relationship with punctilious deference. The corporate machinery is clearly available to stockholders to discipline the order of executive succession. But this unique power rarely is and scarcely can be utilized effectively, short of an open break in management-ownership relations. Modern chief executives—for better or worse—are, as we have said, often in a position to act quite independently of this overriding authority. If they succeed in dominating the board, they can even determine their own successors.

Executives' status as corporate representatives, in this gradually evolving frame of reference, does not require re-emphasis of management's special obligations to ownership as such. However, managers should certainly not, as a substitute, presume to act as representatives of their own self-interest. They are, instead, under obligation to represent the interests of the institution itself.

This clearly is not an impossibility. It is not hopeless to expect civilized men to develop a capacity for becoming identified with a "cause." It happens every day in numerous walks of life. To be capable of this identification is, in fact, the central core of true professionalism. It is the unmistakable sign of social maturity to act impersonally for the good of an institution no matter how this may affect personal ties and friendships.

Owners have, of course, means of redress should they at any time find themselves poorly represented. They have only to bestir themselves collectively. Legal protections are quite specific. Stockholders possess—to repeat—the right of suffrage, often reinforced by cumulative voting privileges and the right of proxy. They have, in short, ample powers, though these are totally ineffective unless used with energy and intelligence. As in all democratic systems, a misappropriated or neglected franchise leads to abuse and confusion respecting the interests of both minorities and majorities. Executives, as deliberate representatives of a well-organized minority, have been known to ride roughshod over a disorganized and inattentive majority just as a willful majority may with impunity be contemptuous of the legitimate interests of minorities.

The democratic way, either in political or in corporate business life, ought not to be held defective merely because the electorate is indifferent. Its strength lies, not in built-in preventives against all chance of abuse, but rather in its means for swift and sure retribution should the electorate become sufficiently aroused by abuses which it no longer finds tolerable. There is no basic weakness in the corporate concept which prevents owners from commanding attentive representation from the executive hierarchy to whatever extent they by their collective actions deserve.

That stockholders are by no means defenseless may occasionally increase the occupational hazards of executives. An aggressively organized minority can sometimes force unwelcome admittance to board membership, thus undermining in this center of influence the confidence which executives must enjoy if they are to survive. This crude intrusion on board-room amenities not only is disturbing to the composure of directorial associates, but is certain to cause harrowing reappraisal, by executives, of their own positions. It is calculated to make them especially attentive to the need for great solicitude in representing the interests of these particular stockholders to others within the corporate complex. Should they fail in this regard, they may be quickly called to account.

An organized insurgency by ownership minorities aimed at creating disagreement within the board itself is—if well disposed and prompted by "the good of the organization"—the natural and constructive means by which alleged executive lethargy and ineptitude become self-correcting. Too often, these intruders upon the board's peace of mind are instead bent upon deliberate manipulation of the company's affairs for personal ends. The chief executive beleaguered by this threat, if he is at all worthy of confidence, must be mindful of his obligations to all vested interests in the enterprise. Even when forsaken by fellow directors whose natural instincts warn them to flee from what may be a painful notoriety, he must choose a positive course to survive. He must rise resolutely to the struggle for ascendency; join forces with his assailants in the hope of eventually wresting some acceptable compromise of motives and aims; or else he must surrender in ignominious defeat with a loss of face and reputation that is bound to undermine his further usefulness as official leader. It is fatal to executive prestige to be incapable or unwilling to lead in time of crisis.

The proxy battle which frequently accompanies these unpleasantnesses, once it gathers a full head of steam, can be a brutal ordeal to any well-intentioned and not wholly insensitive chief executive. It will be doubly so if brought on, not by a gradual accumulation of his own misdeeds and mistaken judgments, but by those of his associates or predecessors for which time has not made amends.

Representing the Corporate Interest in Labor Relations

Executive capacities for sensitive representation of employee interests in corporate affairs usually are much less in evidence than their inclinations to represent the interests of owners—despite the fact that in the modern corporation executives are themselves primarily employees and only incidentally, if at all, stockholders.

One might naturally assume that executives would be entirely familiar and sympathetic with the forces motivating hired workers. After all, their origins and early experience are frequently identified with this group. But for those outside the exclusive executive circle, the fact of common origin or experience tends rapidly to be obscured. To this critical audience, executives are *employers,* not *fellow employees.* Wage earners clearly separate their own class interests from those of management.

This conflict of interest is, in fact, far more significant in wage earners' minds than any vague abstraction having to do with the classic doctrinal differences between capital and labor. To wage earners, if they recognize the parallel at all, executives are capitalists in spirit. They have no illusions as to which side of the bargaining table executives occupy. In comparison with the boss (even though he too is an employee), the shadowy stockholders —the collective owners who are rarely seen and never heard—do not seem very real antagonists in the struggle to share in company income.

Lest customer relations be jeopardized, it is clearly incumbent upon executives to keep in check the incessant demands of both shareholders and wage earners. To favor the one at the other's expense or to give way before both these constant inside pressures at the risk of being gradually priced out of the market can result in no long-run benefit to anyone. Too much preoccupation with the way income is to be shared invariably distracts attention from maximizing the amount to be shared.

Nevertheless, the individual employee thrown solely upon his own resources is without doubt a distinctly forlorn figure in the climate of the modern corporation. He has no formal influence over executives comparable to that of the owners. He has no authorized spokesmen on the board who have direct access to the executive hierarchy, no power of managerial recall if his vested interests are trampled on. If he raises his single voice in protest over some real or fancied grievance, it is immediately lost in the din of conflicting demands or silenced for want of authority. The traditions of his class and a long history of industrial conflict continually remind him that there is no friendly voice within the company itself to plead his case, no open-minded tribunal to right his wrongs.

It is small wonder, under these harassing circumstances, that over the years he should have taken refuge in collective action; that, denied influential internal representation, he should have sought representatives outside; and that his efforts should have taken the particular form they have.

In retrospect, labor's efforts to unite would seem to have been inevitable and, all things considered, to have served wage earners' interests well. But no one who clearly understands the essential dependence of free enterprise upon decentralized economic power, and whose sense of objectivity has not been completely dulled by class sympathies, can derive much satisfaction from certain basic aspects of today's labor movement. Judging by the requisites for maintaining a healthy competitive system, one can fairly conclude that it is extremely unfortunate for organized labor to have evolved in terms of either craft loyalties or broad industrial groups. As these groups have assumed virtually nationwide scope instead of identification with employee interests and aspirations in the individual company, local stresses have built up to almost intolerable proportions. And unfortunately, under the circumstances, labor leaders often are not greatly concerned whether any single company which incurs their displeasure survives or not. The resulting conflict of interest can lead to something quite at variance with the desired goals of healthy competition.

It is quite clear today in the automotive industries, in steel production, on the railroads, in the building trades, in trucking, and—for that matter—in almost any industrial setting one cares to name that modern labor's professional spokesmen have come to occupy seats of enormous influence. The competitive process of selection by which they rise to power, the tightly disciplined constituents they command insure that those who emerge must possess great ability, boundless energy, political astuteness, and a truly exceptional talent for leadership. Their moral strength lies in the validity of their contention that they have indeed helped to right ancient wrongs. Their popular appeal lies in their pose, with some justification, as champions of the underdogs in modern society. Their political potency lies in their ability, the extent of which has long been debated, to deliver the labor vote.

There is no question, in any case, as to the heat and partisanship which the labor problem has characteristically engendered.

The Need for a Community of Interest

No doubt it is to be expected, in an imperfect world, that competition among business enterprises should often turn out to be something less than perfect. Many influences contribute to this, though their individual importance may conceivably be exaggerated by cloistered observers who possibly have never themselves experienced the rigors of competition with full force. Despite our economic system's assorted shortcomings, competition does exist in business in varying degrees of bitterness—as any seasoned executive will readily agree.

But, to preserve this struggle, it is essential that all who become associated with each competing unit—whether investors, executives, or wage earners—be inspired by an abiding community of interest. All must be personally concerned with maintaining their firm's potential for competition. Like a closely knit family with proud traditions, they may fight among themselves, but it is expected that they will present a united front to all outsiders.

The weapons of open industrial warfare are powerful inducements to employers to come to terms. But, when stripped clean of heat and prejudice, they clearly are inconsistent with any sensible concept of efficiency applicable to modern industry. They are almost certain to be abhorrent to the executives of the employing firm, dreaded by many of the employees, seemingly illogical in a well-oriented society, quite devoid of economic sanction, and, if prolonged, bound to be a public nuisance. They are, nevertheless, instruments which a society dedicated to freedom can under the circumstances bar from use only with great reluctance and with serious peril to basic human rights.

There are those who demand that the antitrust laws be applied to labor and industry alike. But there are still others who doubt whether this simple expedient would achieve basic changes in union activities or collective bargaining tactics unless applied with such rigor as to destroy the effectiveness of these essential processes altogether, an alternative of dubious merit.

It is worth recalling that the antitrust legislation of the 1890's provided no special exemptions for union activities. Much later, labor's immunities were defined in sweeping terms by the Norris-LaGuardia and Wagner Acts, although the privileged position thus awarded labor has in important respects since been qualified by the Taft-Hartley and Landrum-Griffin Acts. The outcome of these alternating swings in public sentiment, resulting legislation, and court decisions is that crucial collective labor activities which the courts frowned upon in interpreting the Sherman Act, and later in effect reversed, are again under critical public review. Little has been done, however, to outlaw what unfriendly critics of the modern labor problem call the "monopoly powers of unions."

The real issue as to the applicability of the antitrust approach in dealing with alleged labor abuses may, in the future, conceivably center upon a consideration of means rather than ends. Should, for instance, the attack focus upon structural or functional aspects of the problem? If we assume present union managements are too large and powerful, the remedy could possibly lie, as it sometimes has in notable instances of business regulation,[1] in peremptory restrictions on the size of the union organization. It might, for example, eventually be concluded that a single union management should not be permitted to extend its powers nationally so as to override all corporate boundaries. Or if, in contrast, we assume that certain functional powers which union managements possess are likely to lead to abuses, then a remedy may be amply provided by the injunctive process, which is a reasonably effective legal means of limiting activities and prescribing the circumstances under which they are to be permitted if at all.

The problem of means, as in all social conflicts, can be argued endlessly by men of equal goodwill but different backgrounds and personal loyalties. Solutions to which all can accede and under which all can work with some measure of harmony are, in the end, inevitably reached by compromise. They are almost always resolved, despite the despair of reformers, by a drawn-out process of trial, error, review, and revision.

Co-determination and Employee Ownership

Complete mutuality of interest among wage earners, nonsupervisory salaried workers, and executives as the three distinctive groups of employees in a firm obviously, because of the relationships involved, is most unlikely of achievement.

Stockholders have a special hold upon the executive or management group which insures that their collective interests will not be ignored; they have only to act. Salaried employees in clerical and nonsupervisory capacities are quite frequently in close contact with executives in their place of work. Proximity, more often than not, wins from them (and for them) a reasonable

[1] *Standard Oil Co. v. U.S.* (*1911*).

degree of sympathy and understanding; they generally do not feel they need resort to collective bargaining. However, wage earners typically have no such influence. There are circumstances which prevent this, and which have instead forced them to seek out representatives of their own choosing. Because of their very numbers, collective bargaining is their only recourse.

There are those who have felt this dilemma might be resolved through some provision for employee representation similar to that of the owners on the corporate board of directors. This plan of *co-determination,* as it has been called, has gained some acceptance in European corporate procedure but apparently has aroused little interest in American practice. Indeed, whatever logic it may have in other industrial climates, its acceptance would definitely seem to be precluded by American traditions, both in corporate industry and in the labor movement.

Still others have thought that as dispersion of corporate ownership gained momentum, a closer community of interest among all who are directly concerned might gradually evolve. Corporate employees can also become corporate owners. Fully a quarter of a century ago, scholarly observers of industrial organization were beginning to predict that employee stockholders might affect appreciably the future prospects of corporate enterprise. The sobering effect of ownership, it was thought, might gradually bring about a clearer understanding of the essential interdependence of profit and wages and thus blunt some of the sharper cleavages in the industrial conflict.

The tendency toward influential wage-earner ownership actually seems little more in evidence today than it was then. Recent inquiries seem to indicate that employee-ownership plans may possibly someday become "an integral part of the American industrial scene," though when this will happen or what its effect will be remains undetermined. Only one out of five firms with securities listed on the New York Stock Exchange is reported to offer direct encouragement to wage-earning employees to become stockholders. It is estimated that one out of eight American adults is a corporate stockholder, but apparently the proportion who have acquired equities in the organizations by which they are employed is much less.

Reportedly there are a few large corporations in which the number of employee stockholders is substantial though the proportion of the total corporate net worth which they own is usually quite small. In Westinghouse Electric Corporation, for example, about 30 percent of the employees are said to own stock; in the Du Pont corporate complex, the percentage apparently is even greater; and, in Cities Service Corporation, employees "now comprise the largest single stockholder group." From this fragmentary evidence, it possibly may be deduced that employee ownership is a trend, but in most corporations it is not yet sufficiently significant to have much effect on the objective of providing widespread employee representation from within.

Management's Right to Manage

Whatever the eventual outcome of this issue, there is no grave reason for despair. This present-day domestic conflict between executives, acting as employers, and their employees should be no more beyond solution than equally profound conflicts in times past which have worked themselves out. Two things, above all else, appear to be essential:

1. *In the search for solutions, the conviction must be maintained, firmly and courageously, that it is the exclusive function of the executive command to manage.* No one can fail to recognize that modern wage earners have acquired vested interests in industry rivaling even those of owners. These require recognition and understanding. But neither group's special interests in the corporate entity fit it for management. The executive hierarchy alone can manage. And only at their own peril can executives allow their prerogatives to be whittled away through concessions yielded under pressure. Once surrendered, rarely if ever can they be regained.

Spokesmen for organized labor, whenever they have seen an opening, unfortunately have been quick to insist that they be granted managerial powers. Perhaps their position in its extreme form has never been more baldly stated than by the union president quoted as declaring, in effect, that representatives of labor should have a voice in decisions affecting prices, policies, products made, locations, and the speed at which automation will be introduced—so that hardships and needless suffering may be avoided.[2] The hardships complained of are clearly grievous and deserving of sympathetic understanding. But the remedy has no merit. Sincere friends of both management and labor may venture to hope that the sober position of labor is more accurately reflected in the 1938 statement by Arthur Goldberg[3] that American labor completely respects management's rights and regards it to be not only the right but the responsibility of industry to manage its own plants.

There are few issues of principle comparable to this one. Executives conscious of their responsibilities must be prepared to defend it to the very end—if need be, even under threat of strike.

2. *There must be an unending effort to improve understanding.* Executives must strive unceasingly for a clearer perception of the legitimate requirements and natural aspirations of their workers. Wage earners, in collective bargaining, must likewise strive to understand their employing company's requirements for survival in competition; the function which profits play in its continuing success; the rigorous limits imposed upon the share of income which can be allotted to labor without corresponding improvements in productivity.

More pay for less work is a goal all human beings long for. It has great emotional appeal to executives and wage earners alike but, sadly enough, little promise for either when unsupported by dispassionate economic analysis. Greater pay derived from equitable participation in the fruits of greater productivity, as it is achieved, is the only realistic goal. That these fruits should all find their way into the pay envelopes of labor, as sometimes appears to be contended, is unrealistic. There are other contenders who contribute equally and thus have the right to participate also.

Wage earners, through their chosen representatives in collective bargaining, must present and defend their basic interests with all their might. But management too, through its chosen

[2] From news reports appearing at the time on a 1957 speech by Ralph Helstein, President, United Packinghouse Workers.

[3] Then special counsel to AFL–CIO; subsequently U.S. Secretary of Labor, Justice of the U.S. Supreme Court, and U.S. Ambassador to the United Nations.

executive representatives, must affirm the interests of the company accurately and with the same vigor.

Both must above all see to it that private collective bargaining —always involving compromise on both sides—is preserved. There is no other civilized way, under modern conditions, of holding fast to mutually precious freedoms and still solving this problem that is of such vital importance to the American business community.

V

Executive Functions: Evaluation

THE EXECUTIVE FUNCTIONS OF DIRECTION AND REPRESENTATION ARE invariably concerned with future undertakings. They consist of deciding what is to be done, communicating the decision to those expected to take action, and watching over that action so as to guide it toward intended goals.

But the outcome frequently deviates from what was intended. Unanticipated influences intervene. Numerous factors affecting the result are rarely subject to complete control. Thus it is nearly always necessary to examine the consequences of what has been done, to analyze the causes of deviations, to determine what steps must be taken to put operations back on course. Like the mariner when familiar landmarks disappear, one must be forever looking backward to see that "the wake is straight"!

This process is the function of evaluation. Good executives approach it with critical inquisitiveness, with toleration, with comprehension, with compassion, with a deliberate intention of getting at the reasons for subordinates' actions which may have gone amiss.

Correct evaluation of ideas, events, things, operations, or persons always includes three stages:

1. Gathering, analyzing, and testing pertinent evidence.
2. Searching for valid criteria or standards by which to judge results.
3. Establishing objectivity in formulating judgments.

Correct Evaluation Requires Reliable Information

Systematic organization is required to develop and interpret information about past performance, test it for accuracy and relevancy, and communicate the message to critical points where results can be subjected to unbiased judgment. The scope and complexity of these essential internal "intelligence services" in present-day corporate affairs have created some of modern executives' most pressing procedural problems.

The explosion in scientific knowledge witnessed by this generation has profoundly affected this task of interpreting the results of operations. Applications of mathematics and the physical sciences have become as readily available for problem analysis, evaluation, and resolution in business technology as in other, perhaps more rigorous, intellectual disciplines. The very vocabulary of modern businessmen would have been scarcely recognizable a score of years ago. The list of new tools and techniques for keeping track of what has been done and is being done is long—including, for example, predetermined performance standards, work sampling, operations research, linear programing, mathematical model building, and high-speed data analysis, classification, and retrieval. And most of these we owe in large part to the development of the electronic computer.

There is no question, of course, that bewildering innovations are rapidly becoming indispensable aids to astute executives in the stepped-up tempo of business affairs. The central function of these devices is their capacity to assemble and sort out information with amazing speed. Indeed, they have inspired informed observers to assert that management has suddenly been brought to the very threshold of developments soon bound to overturn traditional concepts of business practice completely.

Predictions—some of them possibly as fantastic as the apparatus inspiring them—imply that, before long, executive actions and evaluations will for the first time be supported by intelligence services and facts requisite for precise measurement and anticipation. Many problems which are now perplexing because they are based upon circumstances perceived only in vague outline will, it is assumed, be solved by completely routine procedures. At the very least, it is contended, the center of emphasis in organization will straightway be shifted from the present decision-making areas in the line to the intelligence-gathering and -evaluating areas of the staff, which will be so self-sufficient in all respects as to make critical decisions automatic and obvious.

But, before we delude ourselves completely, let us remember that these new devices are *only* tools. They contribute immeasurably to the clarification of many operating problems. They summarize data in greater detail and less time but not always at less cost, since data refinements of the precision which these devices make possible may not be needed at all by really astute executives in making many business decisions. In fact, many executives would not use the new data even if they knew what to make of them. As some wag has observed, it is not necessary for a good cook to measure apples with micrometers to make perfectly palatable applesauce.

Intuitive judgments, involving the careful pondering of risks by thoroughly experienced executives, are sometimes superior to "certainty" in cocksure hands even though it is supported by exhaustive factual analysis. The cost of elaborate machinery for assembling data may well outweigh the risks entailed in evaluating a situation and making necessary decisions on the basis of partial evidence more readily at hand. Precision in performance is sometimes indispensable, but in business, as in many other human endeavors which are influenced by prejudices, wishful thinking, and shaky assumptions, it ought always to be justified by something more substantial than merely the appearance of precision for precision's sake.

The glamour with which enthusiasts have surrounded the concept of a computerized existence where all imponderables are presumed to be reduced to absolutes clearly has dazzled many executives. To have a full complement of computer hardware has indeed become a sort of status symbol to which even the front office is not entirely immune. Top executives may not always understand explicitly what they may expect from these investments, but they do understand as well as anyone what it means to be considered up to date.

An attitude of caution is sometimes necessary to dampen the

unwarranted enthusiasm of technicians. Extensive investments in equipment should never be authorized until there is ample assurance that appropriate systems will be provided by which pertinent original data can be identified, checked, and made ready for processing—lest computers succeed only in delivering to management, much faster, information that is essentially misleading. The mysteries of electronic data processing, and the laborious refinements in technique which statistical theorists sometimes indulge in, unfortunately seldom compensate for inaccuracies in the data themselves. The output resulting from these maneuvers is never more valid than the input.

Computer capacity, furthermore, is quite likely to be wasted unless management is thoroughly aware how to use the greatly augmented sources of information to improve business decisions. What is most important is executive determination to do what is needed to correct any dangerous tendencies in operations that may be revealed. Otherwise, reports pile up about which nothing is done. It is not always the executive with the best information services who runs the "tightest ship" in shop and office.

It is indeed a matter of common observation that many organizations equipped with more than adequate information about operations still are deficient in evaluation and control. Reams of statistics and charts without end may be compiled, interpreted, and circulated with monotonous regularity among all who may conceivably be interested. And yet, judged by the resulting action, the reporting services appear not to have been put to very good use.

Perhaps no competent staff executive needs ever to be reminded that it is relatively easy in most cases to analyze a problem, sift from the mass of accumulated evidence that which is irrelevant, appraise the significance of all that remains, and arrive by logical deduction at a sensible solution. But paper decisions themselves are sterile. The real test of accomplishment is to get those who must be relied upon to take action, to secure general agreement with indicated conclusions without first loading them down with unrealistic reservations, to arouse enthusiasm in all who must work subsequently without stint for the project's success.

Such achievement often must wait upon reluctant acceptance by others. It requires patience and leadership talents not always possessed by those who have extraordinary skill in seeing the logical solution to a problem quickly.

Establishing Criteria for Judging Results

The technique of evaluation, when all the essential evidence has been assembled, always involves comparison with valid standards. It is a basic object of science and all applications of "scientific method" to discover criteria by which conclusions concerning phenomena under observation may be tested as a prelude to predicting just what may be expected of them under similarly controlled conditions in the future.

The function of evaluation as practiced by executives in connection with business operations is as much dependent upon the availability of reliable standards for judging things, methods, and performance as are the methods of science. It is noteworthy that 50 or 60 years ago Frederick W. Taylor's distinctive philosophy of shop practice—which later came to be called, perhaps too pretentiously, the "science of management"—was inherently concerned with this problem of standards. The very titles of his classic monographs—"A Piece Rate System," "Notes on Belting," "The Art of Cutting Metals"—reflect the homely flavor of shop practice in the search for standards by which to judge performance. Mr. Taylor and his associates were primarily interested in *things,* but it was in such modest seed beds that some of the most profoundly revolutionizing ideas in modern technology were germinated.

Industrial engineering, as it is known and practiced today, has descended from these and similar pioneering efforts. Its major concern, when it lives up to what it preaches, is application of the methods of science in the development of valid standards by which operating performance can be evaluated.

This search for better standards to aid in business evaluation naturally has extended far beyond the sphere of operating processes and physical resources. Students of social phenomena also have contributed immensely to the serious literature of business since Taylor's day. Modern executives must have a broad familiarity with technology, but this by no means overshadows in importance the need for an equally critical attention to people. They cannot escape the absorbing role of observer, appraiser, manipulator of human behavior; and in this role, they depend heavily upon staff advisers trained in the social sciences.

Social studies, it is true, frequently seem to lack the precise elegance which is assumed to characterize studies of the physical world. Certainty of quantitative predictions in particular, which is rightly presumed to be an essential attribute of scientific knowledge, at best often proves somewhat illusory and inconsistent with our present understanding of human vagaries. Physical scientists and engineers, possibly somewhat smug in the relative assurance with which they contemplate their inanimate world, may be especially fond of such comparisons, but in their candid moments even these critics may have personal misgivings about their own familiar spheres.

Mathematicians, it has been observed, are prone to question each other's assumptions quite sharply when exploring new fields of inquiry; they are inclined to doubt tentatively advanced conclusions until, finally, they have been proved beyond conjecture. Chemists, physicists, biologists—all customarily and doubtless properly subject a colleague's reputed "discovery" to merciless scrutiny before its acceptance and endorsement. Yet at the other end of the spectrum, as it were, of scientific study, it is notorious that economists of equal reputation often use the available evidence to arrive at predictions so much at variance with one another that the public is confused.

It is, of course, the nature of science, whether physical or social, to be plagued eternally by uncertainties. If social scientists have cause for diffidence respecting their accomplishments in comparison with the performance of older scientific disciplines, these defects are doubtless of a sort which time and advancing maturity may heal to some degree. In any case professionals, including scientists, ought always to question each other's conclusions among themselves. For their nontechnical associates, these barbed dialogues may mean little, but it is vital that we be able to distinguish between charlatanry and sound investigation. This is above all important today, when such formerly strange and forbidding fields as anthropology, social and political theory, and especially psychology, along with economics, engineering, and the "earth sciences," lay almost equal claim to an important niche in the disciplined and cultured executive mind.

All these categories of knowledge contribute to the executive's essential task of evaluating things, events, and personal behavior. Economists, even when they do not agree among themselves, are constantly called upon for advice concerning the meaning of events and the state of the economy. Psychologists also have rapidly become trusted advisers in the executive's world; in fact, they are almost as much in demand by the conscientious administrator, continually harassed by the need for accurate evaluations of his associates, as engineering advisers in the realm of material things.

Psychological advisers to management devise standards for judging human accomplishments, give technical assistance in personnel testing, make individual appraisals, provide clinical advice in "problem cases," and hazard guesses as to the chances of success of prospective candidates for positions of executive responsibility. Conceivably, the value ordinarily placed upon these services is more indicative of the extreme importance to executives of the problems to which they are applied than of the general reliability of the advice sought and received.

Everyone who works through people must prejudge and later re-evaluate, as best he can, the probability of success for each of his associates when put to the test. And yet how rarely is this prime executive talent developed to the point of real proficiency. Sometimes, or so it seems, those who fancy they possess it in the highest degree give evidence of having least acquired this precious knack!

In this dilemma, the prudent executive seeks assistance wherever it can be found. He may experience some uneasiness when exposed to the solemn chatter and cautious double talk which typically pervade the executive appraisals which his psychological staff provides. He may readily conclude that what he is being offered is far from a precise technique comparable to what he normally expects from his engineering advisers in their particular specialties. He may fully be aware that these professional judgments of men within his organization on whom he most depends are far from infallible, but so, also, is he! And, if his advisers on personnel do not corroborate his own judgments of his people, at least they prompt him to take another look.

To formulate valid opinions about people, or to assess correctly the results of one's own actions or those of one's associates in authority, demands of executives those rarest of mental achievements—understanding, objectivity, and the courage to set things right. There must be clearly defined standards for differentiating between the good and the bad in performance, warmth and generosity in commending success, persistence in uncovering error, and disciplined and forthright correction of the mistakes by which men learn to improve.

Establishing Objectivity and Avoiding Biased Judgments

Impartial and realistic evaluations, either of persons or of actions, clearly require—in addition to familiarity with all the pertinent facts in the case, plus accurate standards on which to base one's judgment—studied avoidance of all temptation to indulge in wishful thinking. But who can be expected to achieve all this? Men who are themselves being judged or are emotionally identified with others whose performance is under appraisal can hardly be presumed to be totally objective. It is reasonable to expect men in authority to strive diligently to purge their minds of bias, but the probability is strong that to the degree they are personally involved they will be scarcely less influenced by human prejudice or partiality than their associates in the proceedings.

The crucial problem in avoiding bias in the evaluating process is to organize so that this essential responsibility may be shared with others who can act with some semblance of personal detachment. Our U.S. Constitution seeks to resolve this dilemma, though certainly at the cost of some honest misgivings, by a formal separation of powers in the executive and legislative branches of the Federal Government—with particular care to provide independence for the third branch, the judiciary. Impatient reformers may fret at these checks and balances and claim that they cause intolerable delays in dealing rationally with changing conditions. But haste is not really an essential ingredient in social reform, especially when men of equal honesty, equal intelligence, and motives above reproach seldom can agree upon the precise shape reform should take!

The resources and resilience of governmental institutions in almost any circumstances are great. The "coefficient of emergency" in affairs of state is ordinarily of no great magnitude. Despite what reformers may think, it may easily turn out that what needs to be done should be approached with deliberation and caution rather than at headlong speed and at the risk of having to be undone later. The danger here is that, after the lines are firmly drawn, each antagonist tends to become saddled with the self-righteous conviction that he cannot possibly admit to having been mistaken.

In contrast, margins of safety in military or corporate business decisions frequently are exceedingly thin. Emergency situations are always in the offing, requiring sensitive awareness, prompt action, or precipitate changes in direction with a large built-in element of surprise. These times of crisis call inevitably for individualized decision-making authority, but determining the adequacy of the decisions—which eventually ought always to come under review—must, in the final analysis, be left to others.

This process of executive evaluation which necessarily follows the process of executive direction requires special safeguards. By setting the judgment of one against the judgments of others wherever possible, individual prejudices, it is hoped, will be made to offset each other, and as a result a nearer approximation of truth may possibly prevail.

The principle of checks and balances has application here. It is an essential of orderly procedure in all institutional practice, corporate or otherwise. The approach is not through formal separation of powers exemplified in the organization of the Federal Government, but the goal is the same. Every military establishment has its inspector general's department; every well-conceived business organization has its staff personnel who counsel with the line executives and submit the results of line decisions and actions to audit and appraisal.

Occasions where independent checks upon performance are

imperative are readily cited. The list includes, among others, such vitally important responsibilities as appraising the intrinsic merits of end products, controlling quality in production and customer service, measuring performance in shop and office, deciding whether potential customers are worthy of credit, accounting for income and expenses, and searching for errors of omission and commission affecting profit determinations. None of these appraisals can safely be left to shop personnel, sales force, or operating executives—not because these people are indifferent to truth, careless, or incompetent but because, as with all human beings, their own short-run self-interests may sometimes come in conflict with the best interests of the organization.

The purpose of any organized system clearly is to restrain individuals or power blocks from undertakings inimical to the general aims or goals. The necessary check is provided by placing those likely to be tempted by self-interest in positions where their actions will be subject to counterbalancing decisions and actions by others in positions where they are not likely to be so tempted.

By deliberately contrived separations of authority, even though in practice they may seem somewhat awkward, the personal inclinations of one agency—inevitably reflecting some measure of self-interest—are arrayed against those of another, thereby achieving a nearer approach to realistic appraisal. The means of achieving objectivity which are thereby imposed upon operations may slow up action, create duplication of effort, and accentuate latent internal frictions, but the resultant uneasy balance in performance will in the end, it is anticipated, more closely approach the intentions of the organization.

What does it matter if this relatively crude mechanism does fall far short of an elegant solution of the problem? Organizational relationships, dependent as they are upon human motives, never can be made to conform to precise mathematical models, nor do we always want them to—lest the priceless values of individual initiative in unforeseen emergencies be lost. Checks and balances instead function like road blocks, compelling participants to stop! look! and listen! when action begins to deviate from the prescribed course.

These indispensable precautions incident to the function of evaluation are the work of both line and staff executives. They cannot be effective unless the decisions of both are positive and promptly determined. Sometimes procrastination in correcting known weaknesses is a besetting sin of line executives, defeating remedy. But until the cause and nature of the problem calling for solution have been thoroughly investigated—until all conditioning factors have been identified and placed in proper perspective—the decisions and actions of line executives can scarcely be either wise or timely.

To alert line executives to impending trouble wherever it is likely to occur in operations is a major responsibility of the staff. Fortunately, staff judgments can be made in an atmosphere of relative detachment, thus subjecting critical operations at each successive level in the line organization to objective evaluation. But can the same protection against either rashness or lethargy be assured in the heady climate of the chief executive's office where overawing corporate authority resides? To attempt to prevent unwise actions at this high level is clearly a heavy responsibility. Whoever bears it must have the guidance, stimulus, and moral support of the chief executive himself.

The Role of the Independent Adviser

It is, in fact, in providing competent staff assistance at these levels in connection with this function of evaluation that outside professional advisers of integrity, with broad and diversified experience, can be of greatest service to their client executives. Legal counselors, economic advisers, professional engineers, public accountants, industrial psychologists, and management consultants fill this need of modern business.

Unthinking acceptance of tradition-rooted corporate objectives, assumed applicability of policies grown sacred through unquestioned observance, complacent reliance upon performance standards long since outmoded—these are sometimes characteristic of the corporate high command whose members have grown too comfortable in the assurance that their official positions are at last completely secure against attack. Nor are executive attitudes like these complete rarities in many old companies which are still successful in spite of them. Wherever they are found, they need to be subjected to cold appraisal; and independent agencies, competent to analyze and detached in point of view, are in a peculiarly favorable position to do the job.

Like all groups who are striving to establish professional standards of conduct, independent consultants have occasionally suffered from identification with those whose pretensions have not been adequately supported by their performance. But these disreputable elements, there is reason to believe today, are becoming exceptions. Responsible managerial advisers strive to serve their clients by discerning and objective staff assistance. They sometimes are amazed by the fragmentary and inadequate nature of the available information on which their appraisals of operating performance must be based, but they have learned how to ask constructively troublesome questions. Their expert diagnosis uncovers lurking dangers; helps to find the right remedies; and, above all, provides object lessons assisting clients to build effective staff services within their own organizations.

Reputable independent professionals have not earned the confidence of the business community by pretending to know more about a client's business than he does himself. Obviously not. Their special skills lie in mastering the subtleties of influencing people to decide and do what should be done. Like all staff personnel, they must substitute persuasion for compulsion in getting needed action. The experience with many problems in many different business situations which they gradually acquire as they earn acceptance and gain stature stands them in good stead; for, while business problems are always influenced by the environment in which they arise and there is no stereotyped solution which may be applied, they do fall into general patterns which familiarity and breadth of exposure enable the alert observer to recognize quickly.

These independent professionals observe work habits and schedules which permit an intensive concentration upon a client's specific problems which, too often, he himself cannot manage because of pressing and conflicting responsibilities calling for immediate action. Personally detached, they are perhaps not so likely to confuse the trees with the forest as the client may come to be from long familiarity. Above all they can, if they will, remain relatively aloof from partisanship. The vested interests within the client's organization which must be protected; the positions, once taken, which are bound to be stubbornly defended —these should not embroil the outsider.

At their best, independent professional consultants act as needed catalysts, giving sympathetic attention to various points of view, reconciling differences, allaying internal rivalries, seeing that credit is given where credit is due, and in the end hoping to arrive at sound conclusions and evaluations upon which all can agree and which all can defend as their very own.

The essence of good staff work, whether generated from within or without, always lies in uncovering relevant issues and in persisting until the right answers are found. It is the indispensable ingredient in all evaluations upon which effective systems of control depend. And correct evaluation of past performance always is the necessary prelude to any valid progress in future undertakings.

VI

The Organization of Executive Effort

CORPORATE ACTIONS AND REPUTATIONS ARE NEVER BETTER OR WORSE than those of the human agents who create them. For the driving energy in this complex of forces is always executive manpower organized so as to *direct* corporate affairs, to *represent* corporate interests, and to *evaluate* corporate results. These basic executive functions determine in no small measure whether a business succeeds or fails. They are invariably dependent upon people, each insisting upon some degree of individual initiative but of necessity working in close harmony with the others.

It is the task of organization to establish working relations that will promote these ends. The process begins to assume importance the moment the work to be done exceeds the capacity of one man, though a very small group with great mutual respect for, and implicit trust in, one another can usually manage their joint affairs as equals, with a minimum of formality and deliberate prearrangement.

This informality is good as long as it can last. Rigid rules of conduct, essential as they later become with growth, ought never to be established until necessary. They always impose restrictions upon some of the rarer manifestations of the human spirit. In all man's preoccupation with organization, artificial contrivance should never be allowed to hinder needlessly the flights of creative thinking of which some few individuals in each generation of employees are capable.

The essential element of the organization process is the arranging and harmonizing of physical resources and their adaptation to the creative capabilities and energies of the available people in an integrated and disciplined structure. A close interrelationship of individuals, frequently drawn from many origins, must be established. Their respective vested interests in the joint effort must be carefully appraised. They must respond to constituted authority. They must be guided by the needs and be reconciled to the demands of the social order of which the enterprise is a part. It is of first importance that there be a clear understanding of objectives, a precise definition and allocation of individual powers and obligations, a responsible and forceful leadership.

These necessities of organization, if order is to prevail, inevitably affect all aspects of human existence. Every rational being is forever trying to utilize scarce resources to achieve some desired end in the best possible way. This need for systematic organization is universal in social experience and always amenable to analysis and generalization.

In the life of the individual, organization means such mundane things as cultivating time-saving habits, planning activities and attending to them in accordance with a reasonably systematic scale of priorities, scheduling commitments and making sure they are met. In group activities, organization consists of breaking operations into their constituent elements and skills, assigning manpower, devising an acceptable formula of cooperation, opening up avenues for internal communication, establishing discipline, and steering performance toward intended goals. The organic whole, though composed of individuals serving in most instances as specialists of sorts, must act as a single unit. In every institutional setting, organization is depended upon to assemble essential materials and place them at the disposal of selected personnel, with special capacities and energies, who are brought together, given direction, and put to work.

Organization building involves both structure and system. No responsible executive who has acquired some maturity and understanding of how he must necessarily work through people will be inclined to minimize the importance of either. It is through *structure* that internal relationships are established. Available executive resources are thus transformed from an incoherent and aimless group of individuals into a purposeful organism. It is through *system* that a formal communication network is provided, bringing group actions under control. Without structure, no one can be sure what his intended task is. Without system, unplanned operations proceed in unrelated fashion—frequently from crisis to crisis.

Both structure and system must be rigid enough to provide a sense of order, but with sufficient built-in flexibility to encourage those individuals who are capable of independent thinking. Everyone in a position to make a worthwhile contribution should be granted the privilege of a sympathetic hearing and candid appraisal of his ideas by his equals and superiors in the organizational complex.

How to reconcile organizational necessities with individual inclinations is always a baffling problem. It requires an understanding of how decisions are formulated, of how they are communicated, of how resulting actions are initiated and carried through intelligently, expeditiously, and with a minimum of friction.

The process by which the organizational structure gradually evolves is much the same in all forms of group effort regardless of environment—whether in religious, political, military, educational, or other public endeavors; purely private social relationships; or strictly business enterprise. It starts in any cooperating group as operations expand. The first evidences are most likely to appear in elementary separations of task, proceeding from these step by step to further subdivisions as specific activities continue to increase in relative importance sufficiently to make specialization worthwhile.

The reasons behind this gradual evolution of internal relationships are simple enough. It is a natural outgrowth of the principle of division of labor as applied to executive tasks. Effective group action on any appreciable scale invariably depends in part on specialization. Whether in shop techniques involving principally manual dexterity or in the creative thinking of management, specialization begins to yield positive results as the size of the group and the general complexity of the work increase.

Specialization Requires Coordination

This process, however, involves something more than simple division of labor. It almost immediately jeopardizes the internal harmony of the group. Everyone must be reconciled to being placed in a position of constant interdependence. Specialization is essential for efficiency's sake, but it soon becomes meaningless unless there is also some effective way of coordinating the work of the specialists.

The dual objective of specialization and coordination is uppermost in all organizational efforts. The constituent members of the structure must always be clearly identified by analysis of the operations to be organized, but analysis is inseparable from its counterpart, synthesis, by which all elements are sensibly fitted together in a coordinated whole. The accustomed role of each specialist must be specified and respected, but there must also be generalists, so called, who see to it that the specialists do not work at cross-purposes.

The task of the generalists is never easy, for all key members of the group are prone to act as individualists. Each is intent upon diligently exploiting his own skills, and yet somehow it must be contrived that his actions are directed toward common goals. It is the nature of specialization, furthermore, that task subdivisions tend to become narrower and narrower until checked by the rapidly increasing difficulties of coordination.

Almost any complicated task can be subdivided, and the theoretical limits of subdivision are very great. But fortunately the practical limits of specialization in the course of performance usually are easily recognizable, definite, and binding. For example, the process of making a shoe, assembling an automobile, writing a letter, processing a sales order, making a budget, or establishing a policy could in theory be subdivided and parceled out to a much greater degree than is ever attempted in practice.

Why is this so? The answer is clear, even though the precise limit to which subdivision can be advantageously carried is likely to be decided after some trial and experimentation. It is discovered in the process of task subdivision—and much sooner in mental than in manual work—that the promise of added efficiency declines rapidly beyond some critical point. The many specialists begin to get in each other's way, and the difficulties of providing an ordered existence are compounded at a sharply accelerated rate as the number of specialists increases. The goal of optimum economy is finally determined within a loosely defined margin of error by equating the gains derived from specialization with the increasing diseconomies of coordination.

Thus the advantages of specialization, which in modern times have come to be universally accepted assumptions, do have limits. We need to be continually reminded of this. Specialization is a virtue only in the presence of an objective set of techniques and knowledge in which one can become proficient only by concentrated training and practice. If these techniques possess no special quality of uniqueness, to assume that they can best be used by a specialist occupying his own special jurisdiction does not promote efficiency but leads instead to confusion. It is upon the generalists in every organization that reliance is placed to keep in check possible excesses on the part of the specialists.

The corporate executive group which eventually emerges from this evolutionary process depends, then, upon these two cooperating groups: specialists and generalists. The limitations on executive discretion which result from a mixture of the two —the one depended upon to contribute technical proficiency of some sort, the other entrusted with general command—are highly significant. Most executives, when faced with the necessity of shifting base (that is, changing from a technical specialist of sorts to a generalist, or the reverse) are likely to find the ordeal extremely confusing. Heads of specialized departments are generalists only to quite a limited degree and only within their own jurisdictions. Their chief contribution to the joint effort is based upon expertness in their technical fields.

The chief executive, in contrast, is strictly a generalist. He may be less proficient than designated subordinates in any one of the substantive fields under his command, but he must have sufficient awareness of all to weld a multitude of diverse skills into an integrated operation. And skill in coordination is a rare intellectual achievement dependent upon temperament as much as knowledge. It usually is brought to perfection only after first-hand experience of considerable duration.

The Executive Hierarchy

We have seen how the executive group, through its central command, receives its mandate from the board of directors, through which the sources of formal executive authority flow. Taken in its entirety, the resulting hierarchy includes:

- The chief executive officer, who is specially designated by the board for the post of supreme command.
- First-line departmental and divisional executives of more limited jurisdiction, chosen by the chief executive or with his consent to act with specified powers in his place.
- Subordinates of varying categories and ranks at intermediate levels, operating primarily in supervisory capacities.

And, underlying all these at the base of the managerial pyramid, there is the last line of supervision which is commonly referred to as "foremanship" and is especially critical.

The scope and content of the skills represented in this pyramidal structure are obviously quite diverse. The work expected of each successive layer, if it is to be a vital force, must be explicit. Each member of the structure, from the lowest level of supervision upward, takes his special cues from those immediately above until, at the apex of the pyramid, the ultimate source of executive leadership resides in a single individual, the chief executive officer.

This need for placing so great a dependence on one man may be extremely hazardous, but in practice it can scarcely be avoided. Committees, commissions, and boards of control that attempt to act jointly, as equals, in truly executive capacities rarely prove effective for reasons we have already noted.

There are exceptions, of course. The curious theory under which all partnerships operate, for instance, is that partners are equal. Circumstances may require even in this informal environment that there be a "managing partner," but if he is wise he will tread lightly, since his tenure is dependent upon the sufferance of the others. And, as the organization grows and administrative burdens multiply, informal relationships eventually become totally inadequate.

The more formal climate which quickly develops within the central command in the corporate organization almost immediately requires, in contrast, a first in command with unquestioned powers and a recognizable order of executive procedure. Otherwise there is likely to be little spontaneity of performance among those at lower levels. Knowing who is boss is the first organizational requirement for disciplined group action at every level in the structure.

The responsibilities of the chief executive, operating in lonely eminence because of this requirement, are in both theory and practice likely to be so exacting that they seldom are handled with complete satisfaction. Of all members of the organization, the chief executive inevitably casts the longest shadow. He, above all, must maintain a balanced outlook. He must be prudent yet ready to risk heavily whenever a golden opportunity presents itself. He must possess inborn conservatism, be fully conscious of traditions and past values, but always be alert to innovations. He must be cautious yet decisive, not given to procrastination when the consequences of decision are repugnant.

Every chief executive must plan painstakingly, seeking options wherever possible so that he does not become irrevocably committed to a single course of action, come what may. And yet he must be capable of swift action. He must be judicious, aware of the pitfalls but still ready to commit all his resources when the occasion requires it, more concerned with how things can be done than with why they cannot be done.

The chief executive's comprehensive responsibilities require him to be attentive to counsel but courageous in his own convictions once these have been clarified by discussion. He must inspire loyalty but be obdurate in enforcing even-handed discipline. He must be sensitive to the feelings of associates but insensitive to groundless criticism, full of compassion and understanding but able to face the need for sacrificing others' interests when he is convinced the good of the organization requires it.

But where can this amazing array of conflicting talents and traits be found? Men rarely possess these qualities in optimum proportions.

The answer doubtless lies in creating a supreme command surrounded by associates and executive advisers with diverse skills, capabilities, and contrasting temperaments so that they may stimulate and restrain one another. It is in counsel that balanced judgments and actions emerge. The real strength in partnership arrangements, for example, always springs from choosing as one's associates men whose special virtues supplement and strengthen the cause where one's own shortcomings are most glaring. Given mutual respect and confidence—essential elements in all satisfying partnerships—the combination of diverse talents gives comforting assurance of success.

Making Delegation Work

How the chief executive officer in the corporate environment contrives to achieve strength through counsel is determined by the process of delegating authority, which he establishes. He may, for instance, while not relinquishing his position as the primary source of executive authority, choose to devote his own personal attention chiefly to high "corporate business," external affairs, long-term planning, and the like. Internal operations, or specific segments of these, he may decide to delegate to seconds in command who act in his behalf as "assistant presidents"; that is, executive vice presidents, vice presidents, general managers, and the like.

As long as the connotations of this crucial act of delegation are recognized and understood by subordinates, this plan of command is likely to work. The chief must always recognize his own continuing responsibility for his subordinates' actions. He must maintain an intimate community of interest with his associates in the chief executive's office. While appearing to relinquish personal control, he must not hand over the reins completely. The resulting division of general executive power may indeed yield a much more effective central command than if he were to be adamant in holding all that power tightly within his own grasp.

Inevitably, failure by the chief executive to learn specifically how to delegate prerogatives is one important reason why eventually a plateau is reached in organizational growth, stultifying further development and bogging down action while decisions are awaited from the overtaxed office of the chief executive. A recognizable system of executive succession by which the future prospects of the organization are assured is rarely achieved in a stifling and self-generated climate of chief executive indispensability.

Executive authority immediately beneath the central command quickly becomes segmented in any event and assigned to specialists. This evolutionary process, in the beginning at least, is most likely to reflect efforts by the chief executive to seek support in administrative assistants who are qualified as experts in various related groups of activities which are called "functions."

The natural boundaries of these functions are readily identified. Taken together, they make up the total complex of operations. Where conditions remain relatively simple regardless of geography and volume of operations, this functional specialization is by all tests the most feasible base upon which to delegate executive tasks. As the organization matures, the appropriate functionaries tend more and more to be given freedom of action in their various specialties. Product development; financial management; procurement of needed resources; manufacturing; sales and distribution; record keeping, analysis, and interpretation; personnel relations—these represent technical specialties, among others, in which concentrated effort and competence are eventually needed.

Effective Span of Authority

But the creation of functional specialists in top-level positions immediately beneath the office of the chief executive, essential though it is, involves some dangers which need careful watching. The chances are that the process of subdivision, unless resisted, will be carried beyond the limits of optimum administrative efficiency. For any executive acting as a generalist, the effective span of authority—as measured by the number of persons or agencies which directly report to him—has definite limitations.

The dimensions of this span always possess considerable flexibility, to be sure, depending upon subordinates' intelligence and resourcefulness, the capacity of the executive himself to understand and coordinate dissimilar operations, and the general complexity and diversity of the work to be coordinated. Dissimilar and specialized functions, as they increase in number and become more diverse in nature, quickly impose heavy burdens upon the executive who is expected to establish harmony and bring them under control.

This horizontal span of authority—which always carries with it the implied obligation to control the resulting operations—can usually be extended much further without generating confusion when the administrative units reporting to a single executive are much alike. Where they represent stores, plants, or market areas, for example, the task of comparison and hence of control is easier than where they represent, say, sales, manufacturing, financial control, and still other specialties. Common measures of excellence can readily be contrived for contrasting and evaluating managerial actions at different plants. But how can the controller's performance, for instance, be sensibly compared with that of the manufacturing specialist, or the sales executive, or the head of finance?

The difficulty of bringing unlike functions and technical processes into harmony quickly becomes critical. It ordinarily requires that the functional subdivisions reporting directly to the chief executive officer, or to his executive subordinates further down the line, be deliberately restricted in number. Moreover, there are other pressures, real and insistent, which make restricted spans of authority essential. Ambitious men always struggle for recognition and rationalize this urge by insisting that the importance of their jobs requires that they report to the chief executive or, failing this, to as high a level in the hierarchy as they can contrive.

But jobs have no vitality of their own. It is the incumbents who give them this. Their importance and the proficiency with which they are performed are not especially determined by the level they occupy on the organization chart. The chief executive should reserve the distinction of direct reporting to the central command for those functionaries whose areas of specialization play so vital a part in the overall corporate economy as to require his personal attention and direction. He cannot afford to become personally involved in activities and responsibilities which subordinates can assume as well as he.

The Divisional Pattern

Avoidance of burdens which others should bear is, in fact, the reason why—when operations expand, when products and services become extremely diverse, and when markets become specialized—major delegations of comprehensive authority to subordinates begin to be considered by the central command. An intermediate level of generalists acting as division managers is thereby created.

These subordinates are given operating responsibilities of as inclusive a scope as can safely be permitted within prescribed regions, markets, product groups—any area, that is, where specialized familiarity with local circumstances, distinctive production techniques, or unique market conditions is desired. If the newly formed operating units can be clearly separated from one another, then functional specialties—particularly in sales, manufacturing, engineering, and other disciplines identified with local operations—can be assigned as responsibilities of the divisional commands, each within its own jurisdiction.

Some functional activities, to be sure, are essentially corporate in scope. Either economy or the need for uniformity of policy requires that they be dealt with centrally under the immediate direction of the corporate high command. Finance, controllership, personnel administration, and possibly research and development activities are among those which almost always continue to be regarded as primarily corporate functions. True, they may have their divisional aspects as well, but these must be subordinated to broader corporate requirements.

The development of fully fledged operating divisions in lieu of a purely functional (sometimes called departmental) type of organization at the top level serves to bring relief to the central high command. Accountability for performance thus is placed at the point where operations take place in accordance with the principle of decentralized authority.

Responsibility for key functions in these operating and income-generating segments of the business (that is, engineering, manufacturing, sales, local accounting, and local labor relations) can and preferably should be shouldered almost completely by the division managements. It is only when several divisions must use manufacturing facilities in common, for example, or must serve identical customers, or must otherwise, for good and sufficient reasons, share functions that divisional lines of authority become confused and most of the value attributable to divisional independence of action is lost.

Under proper conditions, the divisional pattern of organization at high policy and operating levels has distinct merit. At the chief executive's level, where the burden of companywide coordination is felt in full force, it immediately becomes much easier to secure harmonious interaction among self-contained divisions than to continue under centralized direction specialized and diverse functions of numerous kinds with responsibility throughout the entire corporate complex.

The Shortened Line of Command

The effective span of executive authority can be considerably greater when administrative units are the jurisdictions of divisional commanders possessing comprehensive powers than is feasible when they are, instead, functional departments. And to be able to broaden the horizontal span without jeopardizing control is always advantageous. The relatively "flat" organization structure which is achieved produces an appreciably shorter vertical line of command. For, all other things being equal in the geometrical pattern of the organization, the vertical line of command varies in inverse relationship with the horizontal span of authority and should be kept as short as possible.

Interlevel communication throughout the entire executive structure is greatly facilitated by this shortened vertical line of command. The delays and distortions which inevitably result from relaying information through needlessly complicated and lengthened channels are forestalled. Everyone can act with greater confidence because he is better informed as to the actions of others. Superfluous layers of supervision are not only expensive, they definitely contribute to administrative inadequacies.

Should eventually the number of self-contained divisions increase with corporate growth beyond the effective span, some remedy must of course be found. The most likely step is then to recast operations by introducing a new layer of group executives to whom the division managers, in turn, report. These group executives, when they become necessary, should be empowered to speak with great authority. Their presence lengthens the line of command, it is true, but this can be endured as long as they act for the chief executive without equivocation and with unquestioned credentials.

Any delegations of authority, whether they originate in the chief executive's office or are the work of its group representatives, should if possible always be made in terms of explicit results expected rather than in terms of a specific catalogue of activities to be performed or detailed instructions as to how to perform them. Profit responsibility, for instance, can readily be exacted of division managers if they are qualified and clothed with sufficiently comprehensive authority to control profit performance within their respective jurisdictions. It cannot be exacted within any practical frame of reference from functional specialists. No functional executive ever possesses sufficiently comprehensive authority to accept this obligation. Neither, for that matter, can division managers be held accountable for profits unless they can really exercise control over the predominant profit-determining activities. Product selection, procurement (either through purchase or by manufacture), distribution, cost control, and price administration usually comprise the irreducible minimum if profit responsibility is to be really achieved.

Profit performance, in fact, rarely is satisfactory unless the organization as a whole is deeply profit-conscious, and this objective is greatly promoted by giving divisional executives as wide a latitude as circumstances permit in controlling their own destinies so far as the major factors on which profits depend are concerned. But the requisite conditions must be provided. When division managers are not qualified or lack essential authority to assume responsibility for profits or, for that matter, much more restricted aspects of operations, the presumption that decentralization has occurred is largely a myth.

The Concept of Functional Authority

Many circumstances tend to arise which help to defeat the extremely desirable objective of localized responsibility for local operations. The chief executive himself is frequently tempted, as a divisional pattern of organization evolves, to hold tenaciously to a corporate executive staff with a full complement of functional departments. These may include, at this high level, representatives of strictly operating functions falling within divisional jurisdictions as well as others which are inherently corporate functions; that is, are not readily identified with or performed effectively at divisional levels. The second category presents no difficulty, but the first can readily cause disillusionment in the newly formed divisional organizations.

Corporate executives with functional jurisdictions which encroach upon divisional operations can under the circumstances act sensibly only in an advisory capacity. They must justify their existence, if at all, as technical advisers in their respective roles to the chief executive, as mentors to their counterparts in the divisional organizations, or as oracles of corporate policy in their special fields of competence. Their existence may be wholly logical during the trying evolutionary period when operating divisions are being set up or when specialized executive talents are less than adequate at divisional levels. But, ideally, each divisional organization should as quickly as possible be taught to stand on its own feet. When this goal has been realized, continuing specialized functionaries at the corporate level should be subjected to careful scrutiny.

Corporate staffs of specialists in the anomalous position where they have been deprived of line authority, and thus are devoid of real responsibility for results, tend to become expensive troublemakers. They must be particularly adroit in exerting a constructive but inconspicuous influence upon operations to avoid friction. They represent, at best, corporate overhead which is especially difficult to justify.

Obviously, some functional executives operating in the corporate high command develop exceptional talents of invention and persuasion. They succeed in creating sincere demands for their specialized counsel from operating executives at divisional levels. The staff official who masters this exacting art of exercising *functional authority*—that is, the authority merely to prescribe how matters falling within his specialty should be dealt with—can be of immeasurable worth. He himself may be totally devoid of *line authority*—that is, the authority to enforce his directives—but he is listened to nonetheless. Indeed, he must be credited with an extraordinary achievement in contrast to functional executives, perhaps with equal technical credentials, who when similarly placed dissipate their efforts in controversy with divisional line executives whose performance they are supposed to assist; who bemoan the fact that they have no real authority to enforce their will, build up staffs needlessly to prove their importance, and in their disillusionment make contributions to the joint effort far short of their potential.

This concept of *functional authority* by which staff executives operate, either at corporate levels or further down in the organization, is absolutely essential to a clear-sighted understanding of how large and complex managerial groups contrive to work together. But it must never be allowed erroneously to dilute and undermine the authority of line executives in the eyes of their subordinates. Somehow, executives with line authority and executives with strictly functional authority, whether of equal or different rank, must learn how to live together if the system of executive authority personified in the corporate high command is to win the unquestioned respect of its subordinates.

Vertical Integration of Executive Authority

Organization of executive effort at policy levels must always be closely identified with organization at the supervisory levels of the structure, including, specifically, those subordinate elements that are sometimes, for convenience, called "middle management" and—still further removed from the central command —the borderland between management and workforce which is occupied by foremanship. These supervisory agencies are of vital importance in the complete structure of executive authority. They are the mechanisms by which executive decisions are translated into action. Their vitality and the effectiveness with which they are integrated with overlying policy levels determine, in large measure, any organization's chances of success.

Integration of executive authority from top to bottom is an absolute "must." It also involves a division of executive labor of sorts, but this time in the vertical or interlevel direction rather than along the horizontal planes of the structure. Each successive level in the executive hierarchy actually possesses a jurisdiction which is generally identical with those above and below, but which represents a particular form of specialization appropriate to its own sphere of influence. And, as in all divisions of labor, these corporate spheres must be worked out with understanding and, lest executive resources be wasted, with the express purpose of avoiding duplication. Layers of supervision which have as their major contribution to the joint effort merely the checking and rechecking of the performance of subordinate levels soon find themselves operating in a discouraging atmosphere of rapidly diminishing returns.

How successfully this essential interlevel division of labor is achieved depends upon how wisely those in each layer delegate authority to those beneath. Each executive necessarily works out his own pattern of relationships with subordinates. There is no golden rule for doing this—no completely objective guidelines which mark off unmistakably the relationships which should prevail among an executive, his superiors, and his subordinates. Yet some consistently effective and realistic pattern must be observed.

The higher the level a given executive occupies, for example, the more he should concern himself with ideas and persons. The lower his level, the more he must be concerned with things and actions.

The higher the level, the more an executive should be occupied with general objectives and broad programs. The lower the level, the more he must be occupied with the specifics of carrying out the plans given him.

The higher the level, the more an executive should be occupied with the formulation of policy, the ratification of standards, the establishing of precedents. The lower the level, the more he is necessarily occupied with seeing that policies are observed, standards are met, and precedents are followed.

The higher the level, the more executive time should be occupied with long-run projections and strategies and the development of people capable of making their realization possible. The lower the level, the more executive time must be concerned with getting today's work done—the immediate chores and tactics of operations.

These general keys to the division of executive labor within the hierarchical structure, always far from precise but deliberately contrived and maintained through delegation, are imperative. There is no other way of freeing executive time at higher levels, where executives are few and their responsibilities are burdensome, from the humdrum round of immediate operations. Details and specifics are the natural sphere of lower levels where the executive helpers are many.

Unless the insistent pressures of today's business are shifted to able shoulders further down the line of command, tomorrow's business is bound to be neglected. Planning for the long term, appropriating resources for the fulfillment of these plans, setting operating goals, and assigning disciplined manpower capable of realizing them are necessarily the work of executives high in authority. If these tasks are continually pushed into the background by executive "busy work" which subordinates can do—by every crisis or near-crisis which current operations generate—the future is mortgaged so that the uneasy present may seem more secure.

But how many executives, even among those highly placed in the structure, have mastered this art of decentralizing authority through liberal delegation to their subordinates? How many who succeed in it are able at the same time to maintain the necessary intelligence services which, if deficient, make central control impossible?

This dual need for comprehensive delegation of authority without loss of control may well be the most valid test of executive effectiveness in the corporate high command. Lacking it, executives are almost sure to dissipate valuable attention on routine chores which properly trained subordinates can perform better. Without it, the all-important sense of corporate solidarity disintegrates.

All these divisions of executive labor along both the horizontal and the vertical planes within the organization are meaningful only when considered as interdependent parts of the whole structure. The essentials of coordination can be realized only if the specialists at policy levels and specialists at supervisory levels recognize their mutual dependence.

Cooperation is always a joint responsibility. There must be self-imposed discipline within every free association of intelligent people. They must be determined to understand each other's problems. But this resolve must be strengthened and supplemented by discipline exerted by an overriding system of authority which all participants recognize and obey.

Line and Staff Relationships

Mutual understanding within the structure of executive authority is promoted by still another division of executive labor occurring at both policy and supervisory levels, but especially at the latter. This is the traditional separation of so-called "line" and "staff" responsibilities—a division of executive labor which is mostly subjective in nature and for this reason more likely to cause confusion than is executive specialization in either the horizontal or the vertical plane.

The different functions of line and staff executives are quite distinct and need to be clearly recognized even though a single executive may be called upon at one time to act in a staff capacity and possibly at other times as a line executive. It is the function of the purely staff executive to support those in the direct line of executive command with needed information. It is the function of the line executive or supervisor to decide wisely, interpreting as his judgment prompts the combined counsel of his staff associates.

The need for this differentiation of executive roles has clearly grown out of the problem of minimizing errors in managerial decisions. Conscientious executives always yearn for assurance that all significant factors affecting the wisdom of impending decisions have been duly analyzed, weighed, and digested. The growing complexities of industrial technologies, the increased involvement of industry-society relationships, and the amazing new avenues for problem solving which mechanical fact-gathering devices have opened up have affected the executive decision making process profoundly. This trend is reflected in the composition of the executive workforce by its ever-increasing emphasis upon staff functions.

It is the function of the staff executive to anticipate occasions requiring important decisions by his counterpart in the line. It is his responsibility to gather, process, and evaluate data bearing on those decisions, to analyze his data and construct decision models in advance, indicating what should be done if this or that set of circumstances is found to prevail when the moment for decision and action is at hand.

All these maneuvers the competent staff man must be prepared to undertake with imagination and patience either under the direction of his line associate or, lacking this, on his own initiative. He must recognize that he, as a specialist, views each problem from his own restricted angle of vision. He must expect to work diligently and in complete cooperation with his counterparts in other specialized fields so that the truth, uninfluenced and uncontaminated by either his or his associates' bias, shall in the end be exposed.

He must present his observations and his conclusions completely and articulately with full confidence in their validity. And yet he must recognize that the final decision is not his to make and must cheerfully accept the verdict should the line executive's decision run counter to his recommendations. He must be resigned to the fact that, should his view prevail and prove wrong, he will surely share the blame—but, should it prove right, the credit most likely will not be his but will accrue instead to the line executive whose final responsibility it was to make the decision.

These are heavy demands to place upon anyone, and it is not strange that staff men frequently fall short of expectations. But line men often fail to appreciate or use staff support effectively. Deficiencies on both sides often defeat the intended purpose of staff assistance. Poor staff work is one of the most frequent causes of poor line decisions.

Actually, there is no justification in the tendency still prevalent in many organizations to accord the staff executive a position distinctly inferior to that of the line man. The one cannot function properly without the other. Some men by nature doubtless fit more snugly into the one category than the other, but there is still ample reason to surmise that many young executives in either category, provided they have learned how to discharge their special functions expertly, could probably transfer their skill without too great difficulty to a position of comparable importance in the other. The trouble is that the opportunity is rarely offered. Lateral transfers often are frowned upon because they disrupt the ordinary routine. If a subordinate is capable, his superior is loath to give him up, and the executive to whom he might be transferred would rather not bring in someone who might for a time find his new environment confusing.

Thus this valuable means of training young executives in the making through cross-fertilization is neglected. Staff men are not permitted to grow by cultivating a taste for line responsibilities, and line men have no chance to test their analytical abilities in staff capacities.

Middle Management and Its Importance

The place for this testing process is naturally in the middle management area, where, in any event, the quality of supervision achieved by any organization is likely to be in great measure determined. Despite its critical importance in this respect, this broad intermediate level is usually the first segment of the organization to be cut when retrenchment becomes imperative. Frequently, no doubt, it does provide a safe harbor for prodigious labors of the "make work" variety, but it must nevertheless be depended upon to maintain the essential channels for interpreting and communicating corporate policy to shop and office workforces.

Its staff activities in fact gathering and problem analysis provide an indispensable basis for executive intelligence services at higher levels. It is the main source of tactical efficiency in line operations. It sets up the procedures by which the policies and directives of the high command are eventually translated into scheduled and controlled action. In every well-regulated organization, it represents the seed bed in which potential executive resources are germinated, matured, and made available for promotion as opportunities develop at higher levels.

It is true that the populous middle strata in the executive organization ordinarily contain their full share of deadwood and disappointed hopes. To many, middle management is the end as well as the beginning of their business careers. For always, in business as in all other ways of life, many are called and are full of hope, but few after waiting anxiously are chosen.

Even with this somewhat dreary prospect, however, middle managers contrive for the most part to lead reasonably contented and highly useful lives. Certain it is that these precincts within the organization must be depended upon chiefly to generate the morale and create the environment which will attract young men of promise, give them their initial training, and hold them long enough to fit them for assuming broader and more stimulating responsibilities. If middle management fails in this task, the top levels in the executive structure can never be self-renewing.

Preserving the Integrity of Foremanship

It is distinctly a hazard that this middle management in most organizations constitutes the last level into which the personal influence of the top executives can penetrate with full effect. The lowly foreman at the base of the management pyramid is, in consequence, too often left to man the front line of management alone. In large organizations, especially, his lot many times is an unhappy one, for through no fault of his own he finds himself unidentified—belonging to neither management nor managed.

Since the personal impressions of the official leadership in high places harbored by wage earners tend to fade because of distance, foremen more than anyone else must recreate the image of management which the rank and file see. But how can foremen do this when their own vision is clouded? This is a real problem in any business of consequence.

Military commanders quite properly lay great stress upon the qualities of their noncommissioned personnel. The precision and snap of a unit on the parade ground or its fighting power when once committed to battle is for the time being largely in the noncom's hands. Just so, the tone of operations in mill and shop depends most upon the foreman. He it is who must be looked to for enforcement of discipline, for maintenance of order, for reproduction of the corporate image which the executive high command so anxiously tries to improve. If he lacks training; if he is underpaid in relation to his crew; if he is ill-informed as to the simplest aspects of managerial policy and thinking and must depend on union stewards for his information; if he is dispirited and indifferent about his job and his sense of loyalty and of belonging is shaken by clumsy handling and insensitive superiors, it will be miraculous should these same qualities fail to show up in his men.

This sort of weakness nearly always is found lurking in the maze of conflicting motives and forces typical of the large organization. Only the intelligence and understanding concern of the foreman's superiors can prevent his job from becoming a point of infection. When, in disgust, he wishes for union protection as a substitute for the effective and sympathetic recognition denied him within the exclusive circle of management, something vital to wholesome internal relationships has already been lost. It should be slight comfort to top management that legislation prohibits this form of outside affiliation.

The fact that foreman unionization has long since been outlawed indicates that the problem is by no means new. It is basically one of attitudes. Laws may clarify the issue and place restrictions upon this means of group identification for foremen, but they will not sweep away thinking born of unhealthy internal relations.

All well-disposed men will readily grant that union activities have filled an indispensable need in most nonsupervisory wage earners' lives. Even with all the harassments they inflict upon managers, no reasonable executive in his senses and with some historical perspective on labor-management relations would advocate their destruction. He might justifiably wish that privileges of union membership were forbidden not only to foremen but to special categories of nonsupervisory employees—junior engineers, estimators, time study men, and the like whose vocational instincts should but often do not identify them with managerial interests. But, here again, when this becomes a troublesome issue, executives up and down the line of command likely have chiefly themselves to blame.

In the case of supervisors and foremen, whose interests are clearly identified with management, there is no doubt whatsoever: If they are to deserve this distinction, they must have no ties of loyalty in their vocational environment transcending those to the firm and the system of executive authority of which they are a part. Their superiors in rank ought to expect nothing short of this. However, they themselves must earn this loyalty which is the unmistakable badge of true executive status.

VII

The Question of Executive Control

EXECUTIVE AUTHORITY DEPENDS UPON DEMONSTRATED CAPACITY TO EStablish order in the performance of operations falling within one's assigned jurisdiction. To direct activities and maintain discipline is the essence of control. Lacking the power to do so, executives cease to be executives.

Any business, if it is to prosper in competition—indeed, if in the long run it is to have good prospects of survival—must be sure of its ground in several basic respects. Those who manage its affairs must—

1. Discover and develop a market of sufficient scope and depth to support products and services which prospective customers are willing to buy at required prices.
2. Master the mysteries of innovation so as to keep pace with a dynamic environment.
3. Make sure that operations are productive, maintaining levels of efficiency consistent with those of competitors.
4. Plan and watch over property commitments, both temporary and long-run, so as to earn rates of return on investment sufficient to attract and hold capital.
5. Systemize remedial action to be applied whenever operations begin to get out of hand.

Management's Prime Concern—the Customer

The active forces of commerce, obviously, never are subject to single-handed manipulation. Private businesses may offer whatever legitimate products or services they please, but it is fundamental in competition that no single enterprise ought to be allowed to control the market. Each participant may influence customer choices by almost any wile, short of downright misrepresentation, he chooses to employ; but neither buyers nor sellers ever determine independently and individually what these choices in the aggregate will turn out to be.

No one would suppose, for example, that the demand for any common article of trade—for home freezers or breakfast food, let us say, or for style changes in clothing or cosmetics, aspirin or filter cigarettes, ranch houses or picture windows, to name but a few—has derived from completely spontaneous uprisings of consumers, dissatisfied with their hitherto accustomed way of life. All these commodities are merely samples from an almost endless shopping list, each item on which apparently has profound customer appeal. All, in their progress toward a mass market, have required enormous promotional investment. All require, or are thought by their promoters to require, great annual expense just to hold their own.

But all marketable commodities, to justify great sales efforts while they last, must possess certain inherent characteristics. They must fulfill customer needs of some sort, real or fancied. They must conform with market trends. They must be ''in style,'' as the saying goes. Their sponsors must be quick to recognize subtle economic and psychological changes which are forever destroying established markets and replacing them with something new that is more in keeping with the times. No one would for a moment assume, for instance, that any amount of advertising could restore past levels of per-capita demand for such products as horseshoe nails or chewing tobacco, for whale-oil lamps or high button shoes, for sunbonnets or long underwear. Our museums are filled with articles like these which have given way under pressure to what we call social progress.

Experience thus reminds us continually that business ventures cannot long endure in any vigorous sense without endless innovation. There can never be any relaxation of efforts to develop new and better products, open new markets, devise better ways to produce existing products. To imitate the lead of more venturesome and resourceful competitors is hardly enough in a free market. The parasite who lives by copying the work of others never really accomplishes much beyond spoiling the market for his model, who already is reaching out for new and better ways of serving his customers.

This general urge to excel is beyond a doubt the basic virtue of the free market system. It provides powerful incentives to create. No other system so surely and ruthlessly exposes mediocrity. The great economic challenge of our social order is how to preserve these values inherent in our system. Eternal vigilance and profound understanding of its virtues and requirements are widespread necessities if we are to avoid setting in motion (or permitting to be set in motion) forces leading to its destruction.

Executive complaisance, inspired for the time by the comforting appearance of black ink on the profit statement, by precarious industry leadership, or even by delusions of permanence, is the great weakness. It has often converted tradition-ridden enterprises with much outward show of strength into what is presently found to be a hollow shell. Gradually declining profits make their creditors aware, eventually, that the risk they have assumed is no longer what it seemed. Suddenly it is discovered that the business in which they placed their confidence has lost out in the savage struggle to survive, that it can no longer face up to the sunlight of competition. Examples have a way of appearing on the business horizon with deadly regularity year in and year out.

The Strategy of Sound Innovation

Successful innovation depends upon a great deal more than personal hunches and lucky strokes of fortune. It is likely to be based instead squarely upon the habit of endless investigation. To embark on an expanded program entailing the normal addition of complementary items to the existing family of products

—or, even more critical, to undertake diversification or new ventures unrelated to present operations—involves far-reaching decisions. Once made, they are not easily reversed.

Ordinary prudence thus requires that all innovations first be put to the test. Proved performance provides essential insurance before submission, full blown, to the discerning judgment of the marketplace. Product development and selection can never be consigned solely to engineers, to production experts, or to sales forces.

New products always require, to be sure, engineering endorsement as to consistency with approved design standards. They require the approval of the manufacturing staff to give assurance that production costs have been accurately projected. They need to be reviewed by experienced sales personnel to insure that covering these costs will not result in pricing the venture out of the market. But there is no substitute for actual consumer approval, or for candid market analysis to establish in advance how much of a market may be expected at necessary price levels.

These indispensable counterparts of fruitful product research and development are most difficult to achieve. Attempting to measure probable market potential for products not yet much beyond the conceptual stage requires an exceedingly hardy prophet. Many things can render the forecast useless. Everyone who is experienced in these matters can readily recall case after case where large sums of money have been spent in bringing new product ideas to the prototype stage of development before the shocking discovery that few customers are going to buy, at least at the price the product must carry to cover costs.

The engineers may be enthusiastic—intrigued by the technical principles involved in the proposed design. The manufacturing organization may find the prospect of utilizing idle machine time or providing employment for productive labor hours attractive.

The sales force may be optimistic because the proposal gives promise of offering something in advance of competition. But the product may be overdesigned or too costly, or customers simply cannot be found! Expensive research and time-consuming experimentation are written off, all because someone in authority has forgotten that competitive enterprise lives upon customer approval. A competent student [1] of research activities has observed that the process of innovation by which scientific discoveries are translated through technology into the economic life of society in the form of goods and services is one of the greatest challenges confronting the free enterprise system. In no other environment, surely, does so much hang upon downright inventive achievement.

But fruitful research in any surroundings is clearly dependent upon organization. It entails careful planning of operations. It is a problem, first, of focusing the attention of competent research personnel upon the desired object; second, of projecting the anticipated market, the share of the prospective demand which can probably be captured, at what cost and with what anticipated returns, as the result of proper selling effort; and, finally, of estimating the likelihood of offsetting losses through replacement of present products. Nothing is gained by needlessly undercutting an already established product, for the moment secure because customers are satisfied.

All these preliminaries are directly related to the research which must precede the basic task of converting laboratory discoveries and factory prototypes into practical market applications. This next step, too, is beset by uncertainties which require caution. Many product developments which have passed every laboratory test turn out to be abortions; they are discarded in the shop or, worse still, much later in the market. To act quickly is urgent, for the project that is finished first has the advantage of an early start, but to act prematurely can be fatal.

Errors in design or misconceived objectives which are discovered and corrected forthwith are much less costly than those which have to be corrected after resources are already committed, promotional efforts have been launched, and distribution pipelines have been filled with unacceptable merchandise. All concerned need to be reminded continually of how many times, even in the best of companies, new products have to be recalled or costly parts replacements and service have to be undertaken for disillusioned customers in the field because of avoidable miscalculation somewhere in the organization. The reputation of

---

[1] Mottley, Charles M., "Managing Innovation for Growth," *Stanford Research Institute Journal*, Vol. 5 (1961).

having produced a "lemon" in the anxiety to be first is a distinction never easily lived down.

There are major lessons in strategy to be learned from this problem that is common to nearly all progressive enterprises. The decisions entailed in launching innovation have broad ramifications. They are corporate in scope, involving interdependent specialists in every field of activity: research, engineering design, manufacturing, distribution, and finance.

The process by which sound innovation is decided consists of two phases: preparation and action. The first necessarily is characterized by indecision. This preliminary phase consists of investigation, of pretesting, of planning, of looking searchingly at alternatives and weighing their relative merits judiciously, of systematically narrowing down comparisons to the point of choice. All these preparatory maneuvers are essential aspects of the fine art of executive decision, which, it has been aptly observed, "consists in not deciding questions that are not now pertinent, in not deciding prematurely, in not making decisions that cannot be made effective, and in not making decisions that others should make." [2]

Both in this cautious time of preparation and in the second phase of the innovation process—the time of action—informed alertness is all-important. "Great decisions which make great commanders," whether in the profession of arms or the civil pursuits of peace, as Winston Churchill somewhere once explained in an analysis of world war events, become so for two reasons: the care with which the plan of operation has been worked out; and the commitment of resources to its fulfillment. These resources, always in scarce supply, must be carefully husbanded and, as much as safely can be contrived, held in reserve. For when once completely committed, nothing further is possible, save to await the outcome as calmly as one can.

The time for action requires that all indecision be brusquely thrust aside. Everyone concerned, with whatever resources the organization can make available, must in the end be committed, if needed, to the prospect of success. When the campaign is fully launched, there is "no substitute for victory." Halfhearted

[2] See Barnard, Chester I., *The Functions of the Executive,* Harvard University Press, 1938, p. 194.

measures, whether in introducing new products and services, in gaining acceptance for those already offered in the market, or in struggling to produce them at less cost, are self-defeating. They are never quite good enough. More determined competitors, unfortunately, will eventually win out. Progressive loss of position in one's established market is always the clearest evidence of impending disaster.

Maintaining Productivity Levels

Ability to meet competition, or the lack of it, is sooner or later dependent upon characteristic levels of productivity maintained in internal operations. It is the prime objective of management to be efficient, and efficiency is measured by comparing the productivity levels actually achieved with some standard representing management's performance goals.

But the concept of productivity has different meanings to different people. In the shop environment and among wage earners, it ordinarily means how hard one works and to what purpose. It involves physical energy, personal skill intelligently applied, willingness, emotional stability, environmental aids or deterrents. The degree of performance achieved is likely to be expressed in shop parlance as so much output per man-hour.

This oversimplification is somewhat unfortunate. It mistakenly suggests the popularly accepted idea that improvements in productivity are attributable mostly—if not altogether—to how hard men at bench or machine have worked and how intelligently and willingly they have applied their energies to their jobs. This granted, it is easy to reach the next fallacious conclusion that the wage earner is, in all fairness, entitled to whatever cost advantage may accrue from improved productivity. If wage increases equal this advantage, the incentive to make a further investment in the interest of improved efficiency disappears. Should they exceed this advantage, the result is either inflation or declining profits.

Of course, it usually can be readily demonstrated that the individual worker's "put-out" at the precise point where value is added in manufacture has little bearing, above some optimum working pace, upon the improvement trend in shop output. The skill required of him and his responsibility for operating more effective tools may have increased, thus justifying increased compensation, but the tools themselves and the supervision he receives have clearly become much more important in determining output.

It is commonplace, though frequently ignored, that the capital investment per direct worker continually increases many-fold. This undoubtedly reflects in part the substitution of mechanical power for human brawn. But, even more, it represents a transfer of skill from the machine designer and builder to the tool's edge, as it were, downgrading in the process the need for craftsmanship on the part of the man who works directly on a product which once, supposedly, was his pride and joy.

In many industries, as is well known, this per-capita investment amounts to $25,000 or more—possibly twice as much as a decade or so ago. Manifestly, in testing the validity of contemplated technical changes from the standpoint of their bearing upon improvements in productivity, the anticipated output per dollar invested may be just as significant as output per man-hour.

The concept of productivity and its causes in modern industry is actually a very complicated affair. It is the result of interaction between such extremely diverse factors as the skill, energies, and morale of workers; the rate of replacement and availability of capital for investment; the state of the arts of engineering resourcefulness; the price of labor and the rate of interest; solicitous attention to customer wishes and the fickleness with which people turn to something new; the volume of required production and the vagaries of the product mix; the accuracy of predictions and the adequacy of plans; the timing of action, the alertness of supervision, and the promptness with which operating results are reported; and the discipline and sense of order imposed upon performance.

All of these factors influencing productivity boil down in the end to two fundamental criteria of successful operation: how well customers believe they are served, and at what cost they are served. (Unless the consumer benefits eventually from technical progress, where is its social advantage?) If the company's performance as measured by these criteria compares favorably with the best that competitors can do, management need not be especially anxious about either productivity or profitability. The goal of controlled operations has been brought within range, though to keep it so requires eternal vigilance.

Dangers of General Impressions

Many of the misconceptions which plague management and cause operations gradually to get out of control arise from drawing conclusions from impressions too general to be conclusive. The broad statistical averages from which executives frequently derive comfort usually are not very reliable bench marks for tying in operating projections.

It may seem reassuring, for example, to know that average gross margins are not much out of line with industry performance; that profits on sales and investment have been fairly stable even though not as good as might be wished; that the record of sales expense and the company's share of the market compare reasonably well with rumors afloat about competitors' achievements. But what about the fact that a more penetrating inquiry reveals that 2 percent of the customer list yields 80 percent of total sales, accounts for 70 percent of gross margins, and requires only 10 percent of selling expense? Is it not disquieting to learn that 15 percent of all the customers, let us say, yield a mere 5 percent or 10 percent of sales dollars, require 30 percent of direct selling expense, and contribute only a token amount to gross margins? What about the unsettling revelation, to probe still further, that some markets in which a position has been taken suck up very substantial proportions of total sales effort but yield no profit? That 10 percent of the field sales force do not generate enough volume to pay their salaries?

These questions are not altogether hypothetical because they do in fact reflect circumstances or approximations thereof found frequently enough in practice. The point is that comforting general averages arrayed against even simple analysis begin to seem less meaningful. If organization and control have as their goal the utilizing of scarce resources to good advantage, sales effort—which is always scarce—possibly can be better directed.

Intelligent sales management is the key, but where should efforts be concentrated? A thoroughgoing examination of actual customer lists and of market areas from which sales orders flow is only a first feeble step toward this objective. Sales analysis is one of the most elementary concerns of market research. At best, it merely fills in the precise details of what has already happened, yet how often even this is neglected! And what about market potentials calling for new and more intensive cultivation? About product testing and the probing of customer preferences? About predictions on which to base future plans, realistic sales targets, and defensible standards of performance?

Opportunities for constructive market research in these areas are, in many organizations, virtually unlimited and untouched. So much depends upon long-run planning, for example, and yet to predict demand as much as a year hence, with sufficient accuracy to provide guidance, is often the despair of sales and operating executives alike. To project sales so far in advance— surely not an unreasonable requirement in most businesses if broad operating plans are to be laid out—requires a very special gift of prophesy. It can at best be achieved only within very loose limits. The result is bound to cause the perfectionist acute distress, but he must find what solace he can in the realization that the best plan that can be made, crude though it is, is better than no plan at all.

Fortunately, the case is not hopeless. Some managements have found that predictions of market abnormalities can gradually be brought into focus by systematic review and progressive revision month by month. Vision becomes sharper as distance diminishes. As the need for accurate planning of lead times and positive control of current production becomes more pressing, estimates of sales requirements can be refined and accepted with greater assurance. Thus the final revision, at most one or two months in advance, will in the nature of events have all the preceding guesswork squeezed out of it and will have substituted firm commitments. It will have gradually ceased to be an educated guess and become instead a shipping schedule sufficiently reliable to serve as the pattern for intended deliveries.

This process, when supported by categorical analysis of product volumes, of regional expectations, of whatever detail seems important, clearly provides a much more adequate basis for control than sheer crystal gazing, unadjusted historical patterns, or general averages of past experience modified by hunches or the state of the forecaster's digestion.

The sedation afforded by normal performance or past laurels is a prevalent danger in every aspect of operations. The general average, provided it conforms with precedent, is a bench mark of sorts from which to start. But average performance cannot be improved by a frontal attack.

Take inventory control, for example. How significant is it to know that so many tons of inventory, worth so many dollars, which turn over on the average so many times a year, are lodged somewhere in the category called "inventories" in the working capital accounts and stored somewhere in corporate warehouses or assembling yards subject to the ravages of rust and weather? Are these general impressions, although expressed in numerical totals with reasonable accuracy, of help in controlling inventory investment? Not very much, surely. And yet instances have been observed where generalities such as these were about all the information which could readily be drawn from company records of dollar inventory amounts in nine figures! Naturally, more information was available, but it was scattered about—and, for all the use made of it in effective control, it might not have existed.

The managers concerned were not stupid. On the contrary, they were sorely troubled about bringing this large commitment of capital under control. More figures, obviously, were needed. But people are readily appalled by the prospect of increasing what already appears to be a very large and, they fear, unjustified burden in clerical forces and data-processing equipment.

In these fears can be seen evidence of a deep-seated tradition. Executives have become accustomed to spending many millions for plant equipment. Competition seems to require it. But to spend much more modest sums to modernize the system of communication and control so that these larger property investments can be used to maximum advantage is a prospect to which they have not become so accustomed.

This apparent inconsistency is not totally irrational. Modern office hardware and the clerical payrolls which accompany it can be enormously useful when properly applied to inventory control or, for that matter, any other problem of control where large blocks of numerical data must be assembled, classified, and summarized in meaningful terms. But hardware investments and clerical payrolls, until brought under control, are only expensive overhead. They are useless until they are integrated in a system which executives understand, know how to use, and adopt as their very own. These tools and the men to operate them can readily be acquired, but it takes time to indoctrinate management in new attitudes and in the use of the unfamiliar records and reports thus produced and incorporated in the system of control.

Good inventory management, possibly more than any other factor in production, involves working with enormous detail. It can make or break many a business. It is easy, for instance, to demonstrate that proper inventory turnover is the very heart of successful merchandising. Retail managements have long since recognized this. But their sophisticated methods of controlling inventory would strike many industrial executives as intolerably burdensome. Industrial sales personnel in particular sometimes seem to have no more than superficial interest in inventories and their control except when shortages prevent prompt deliveries.

The blunt truth of the matter, whether in trade or in industry, is that either inventories work for management or else management finds itself supporting the luxury of useless inventory dollars. Sometimes accumulations are out of all proportion to any conceivable need. The only real justification for inventory investment in the industrial plant lies in reconciling product availability in the market with the practicalities of economical and timely production. Slow turnover can sap the profit potential of any business if the basic facts about inventory behavior are not known or available to the right people in sufficient detail to permit intelligent guidance.

To maintain balance in the inventory investment and to be able to anticipate variations in the product mix in which are hidden numerous exceptions to the general averages which characterize the inventory account in total—these are the important things. But inventory management by which proper balance is maintained too frequently becomes everyone's business. No one seems to know very precisely just what quantities exist, just where they are, just how salable they happen to be, or just what ought to be done about them.

Centralized control of inventory details is not impossible with modern mechanized data processing—indeed, it is imperative. For good inventory management requires knowing what is wrong about present inventory commitments and—more important still—fixing explicit responsibility for action. Somewhere someone must see that realistic standards, not in terms of massive inventory aggregates but in terms of specific item categories, are provided and that exceptions are investigated.

Control Based on "Exceptions"

It is only in dealing with specifics which run counter to the average that correctives become fruitful. It is the exceptions which count most.

Frederick W. Taylor [3] many years ago pointed out the importance to management of events which deviate from the regular pattern of operations. By focusing their attention on variances from past averages or standards, executives are spared the time-consuming task of reviewing corporate or individual performance in detail. Thus they are free to consider questions of overall policy and to guide and counsel the men under them in broad terms.

Actually, application of this "exception principle" is the thing which makes managerial control possible under modern conditions. Otherwise, executives quickly are overwhelmed by detail.

Good Staff Work Plus System

These elementary facts of existence link effective control unmistakably to good staff work extending into every division and

[3] Taylor's *Principles of Scientific Management* (Harper & Brothers, 1911) lists the exception principle as one of the elements in the management "mechanism."

department of operations. Technicians trained in special tasks and line executives who appreciate and know how to use their services are needed at every point.

How, to be explicit, can the efforts of workmen in the shop, of clerical employees in the office, or of salesmen in the field best be organized? How can their compensation be kept equitable? How can they be given realistic goals and realistic standards of performance which will spur them on? What numerical relationships between direct and indirect workers of various categories can be defended? Where can overhead be cut? Are costs responding with anticipated sensitivity when volume is declining? How are equipment replacements and plant investment renewals determined and systematically scheduled?

These questions are by no means academic. Some of them are being asked by alert line executives every day. They can be answered by a competent industrial engineering staff. Indeed, the adequacy with which they are answered often can mean the difference between success and failure—between control and disorder.

Yet how often is the industrial engineering staff accorded a status commensurate with its importance? How often are industrial engineers among the first to go when reductions in force are ordered? How often is this vital activity threatened with extinction when standards of wage-earner performance set by sound industrial engineering research are shockingly disregarded and thoughtlessly negotiated away under pressure at the bargaining table?

But let us look at another area, equally sensitive, frequently fully as baffling, seldom if ever controlled to the complete satisfaction of serious executives. How, for instance, can sales expectations and plant capabilities and intentions be reconciled? How can communication be systematized sufficiently that sales orders can be quickly translated into realistic plant schedules? How can valid delivery promises be made and consistently honored? How can the sources of information on orders in process be organized on the exception principle? There are usually, after all, relatively very few orders among thousands which in the beginning are threatened with real trouble. How can these few be unerringly spotted and quickly put back in the groove before delays become so serious that they throw the whole schedule into disorder?

These are the issues involved in systematic production planning—providing that, in practice, it can be lifted out of the category of frantic expediting. Too often this function deteriorates under pressure into rushing from crisis to crisis but never quite catching up with broken promises before customers themselves inquire when they may expect delivery on shipments already overdue. But these problems clearly are not insolvable. Effective systems of production control have been devised under extreme difficulty often enough to justify attack on this vital service to customers with complete confidence. Production *can* be controlled. The system appropriate to the circumstances is the important thing.

One point is certain: There is no problem of operating control for which some ready-made remedy is the perfect answer. All organizations are very special cases. The solution must always be shaped to the local scene, though the kinds of problems demanding management's attention everywhere are much the same. In any situation, failure to find good solutions should cause acute dissatisfaction and a new resolve to seek and apply correctives.

The task of devising an effective system of operating controls is extremely complex. It includes such diverse aspects as control of sales effort and market coverage; of working capital investment and inventory management; of customer service and the flow of products through the plant; of product quality and spoiled work; of maintenance programs and housekeeping standards; of plant properties and rational treatment of obsolescence; of the orderly scheduling of equipment replacements and renewals; of the planning of cash flow so as to keep finances sufficiently liquid. Whatever the problem, the objectives of the system are the same: the correction of current difficulties, surely, but—much more significant—the prevention of recurrences. Permanent correction is fundamental. Patchwork treatment, which so often takes up much executive time, is equivalent to no system at all.

Do customers complain, for example, of product failures? Do

the costs of product spoilage seem exorbitant? When new products are first introduced in the shop, does turmoil invariably result? Does the time required for shaking down operations, making necessary design changes, achieving standards consistently, and similar annoyances nearly always prove excessive?

The chances are that the system of quality control is defective. Inspection procedures can be devised which keep within bounds the slipups which, with exasperating frequency, misdirect substandard work to the shipping dock rather than to the rework department. The reasons for repetitive failures can be analyzed. Exceptions can be identified; and corrections, where necessary, can be initiated.

Systematic "tear down" procedures applicable to new products and "first runs" are merely common-sense preventives which always can be established without prohibitive cost. Mistakes in design, faulty tolerances and finishes, wrong specifications can be discovered in this way. Engineering changes can be made; drawings can be corrected; shop instructions and special precautions can be noted. There is never any very good excuse when a long record of costly engineering change notices ("ECN's," as they are usually called) follows the introduction of a new product into the shop for months on end.

Good control costs money, but it is not nearly as expensive as spoiled work and the reputation among customers of not being a "quality house." It requires centralized responsibility; it requires inspection facilities and procedures capable of detecting deviations from acceptable standards, and that right quickly. It is principally a matter of executive attitudes: willingness to recognize product failures even when one is certain to be blamed personally and one would much prefer to cover one's tracks; and unquestioned authority to enforce corrections.

Planned Property and Investment Maintenance

Property maintenance is still another large item of operating cost for which the standards of control frequently leave much to be desired. This is always one of the relatively critical areas in plant operation. Maintenance work is extremely variable, and supervisors are prone to excuse failures by doubting whether the techniques of control readily accepted on the production line really apply here.

Experts insist that this negative response is mostly delusion. Standard times for all the ordinary routines involved in keeping machines running and housekeeping under control can be determined, and manning tables can be established. Repair operations, other than those which result from breakdowns and are always exceptions, can be scheduled. Emergency stoppages can be minimized through systematic inspection. Spare-part requirements can be anticipated and needed stocks laid in and indexed for ready reference before breakdowns occur.

Discipline, above all, can be enforced even though maintenance forces move under orders to the remote corners of the plant. A well-thought-out maintenance system invariably results in substantially reduced costs; and better still, when its objectives are explained and understood, it is usually accepted without great reluctance by the workforce. The morale of intelligent workmen seldom suffers from the understanding that management in all fairness proposes to enforce discipline and establish order.

Probably nowhere in manufacturing operations is tight control so likely to yield good returns as in dealing with property investments. It is frequently said that in many industries—even in industrial America!—much of the existing plant is outmoded. This could be for any one of a number of reasons. Perhaps financial stringencies do not permit what is thought to be the luxury, even though it is economically justified, of extensive plant renewal. Or it may be that labor's attitude discourages renewal, fully aware that, should extensive replacements occur, the processes of automation will be hastened. Or management may harbor the delusion that it is enjoying the benefit of a property investment fully depreciated; that "making do" with the present patchwork plant is providing an extremely attractive operating-cost structure.

Costs, for the time being, can be covered up and deferred even though in the long run there may be a rude awakening. Well-meant accounting conventions often delude us. Frequently, too, no one in remote control really knows how bad the plant actually is, or how soon the new investment might pay for itself in spite of negligible depreciation charges on present equipment.

Obsolescence is a mathematical concept. It can be determined as precisely as is permitted by the accuracy of the estimates used as quantifying factors in the equation stating the problem. It is not dependent upon the age, capability, or state of repair of the facilities themselves. It cannot be determined by visual inspection. It depends instead upon objective economic analysis of accurate cost records and realistic engineering projections.

The first requisite for intelligent control of property investment, therefore, is a detailed and exact historical record of property accounts. This must assemble for convenient analysis precise information on what facilities are available in the plant; what their condition and capabilities are; what they cost to operate; and how this cost compares with available options capable of providing equivalent or superior service. These computations are the only real basis for a sound equipment-replacement schedule. Unless such a program is planned and activated, the property accounts can scarcely be said to be under rational control. Financial requirements for orderly replacement schedules cannot be foreseen; important costs may be hidden or not what they seem; competition may gradually gain ground without anyone's knowing just where the competitive advantage lies.

In all these broad areas of operations, which no doubt could be added to almost indefinitely, it is possible to see the essentials of systematic control of operations. The process is always the same. It depends upon understanding clearly—and thinking through in advance—both ends and means.

Control Begins—and Ends—with a Forecast

Control invariably starts with a plan. This is necessarily linked with what has gone before, for its object is prevention in future operations of undesired tendencies reflected in the record. The planning process, to be constructive, must embrace especially those activities and events which are capable of significant improvement.

Effective planning of activities eventually culminates in a "performance budget" embodying managerial policies, summarizing expected end results, documenting the program by which it is anticipated that these end results will be achieved; and, ultimately, showing what the result of these projections is likely to be in terms of profits, anticipated return on invested capital, and the prospect of survival. It requires, in the final summation, a forecast of anticipated income and expenses.

Preparation of this forecast is the first as well as the last requirement in the budgetary process. As has appropriately been observed,[4] it should be regarded as a method of thinking about the problem rather than the answer. The object is not merely to prepare an estimate of future expectations but to identify the variables and ponder over the probable nature of their import. As new data come in, the statement provides a basis for continual reappraisal of the situation resulting progressively in a firming up of conclusions the closer they come to realization.

It might be argued, of course, that a forecast or budget set up as a target for operations but subjected to progressive adjustment and, possibly, retreat from original objectives when confronted by changing conditions beyond control is hardly a reliable guide to success. Of what value is so uncertain a budget? If the objective is to be modified whenever circumstances indicate that performance is deviating from expectations, what is the point in setting a goal in the first place which is so unlikely to be achieved?

The justification lies in the fact that the processes of adjustment which occur are twofold. The target itself is adjusted—downward should it become clear that it is no longer tenable, upward if conditions improve. In the meantime, operations are modified and re-aimed in the direction of the new target as circumstances require.

Control is never simply a process of setting objectives and hoping they will be realized. Conformity with valid expectations, which is the test of control, is never absolute; but neither does

---

[4] Schultz, George P., Dean, School of Business, University of Chicago, in some remarks introducing a panel discussion on "The Business Outlook" before an alumni group.

the prospect of achievement depend completely upon chance. It consists instead of the nearest practicable approach to the possible. Executives must do the best they can in an environment in which other powerful influences besides their own are always present. But what proves ultimately to be possible is no more determined by these outside influences than by the executive's ability to appraise them at the start and to bend all efforts toward softening their effect.

The intended goal, to be satisfactory, must always be a specific and positive one. The budget which projects a loss from operations without resulting in serious reappraisal and constructive planning as to precisely what must be done to replace that loss with a profit is surely no guide at all. Whatever may be the political philosophy which condones and justifies deficits in governmental budgets year after year during good times and bad, it is certain that this provides no valid pattern for private corporate affairs. Deficits may be unavoidable in the new firm, but the dolorous projections must be reversed at the earliest possible moment. Limited corporate resources permit no other option.

Budget expectations provide standards with which to measure progress and compare performance. But these standards by which progress is measured should never be stationary or treated as though they were immutable. A flexible budget—and no other is worth much in a changing world—is based upon moving targets which respond sensitively to the influence of dynamic programs designed to meet and, if possible, improve upon the original expectations.

It is essential that executives be determined to make things happen. Final budget approval by the chief executive should always depend upon a single test: Will this proposal achieve the intended result? How it is to be accomplished can then possibly be left to subordinates. Their accountability for means to the desired end should be explicit.

Suppose, for example, that sales executives submit a budget inconsistent with known market potentials, promising less than satisfactory profit margins, conceding a position of unjustified superiority to competitors, projecting a quite deficient plan of market coverage. The architects of such a program clearly must bear the burden of proof in justifying their proposals. The occasion requires at the very least a searching diagnosis of existing shortcomings and a positive schedule of corrective action. Price policies will probably need to be reviewed, product capabilities reappraised, market outlets reinforced. Until these probabilities have been exhaustively and constructively examined, the proposed sales budget is not worthy of approval.

Or, to cite another example, suppose that payroll budgets appear excessive in relation to anticipated output. Is it not imperative that, before approval, remedies be developed and applied? Projected manning tables covering key operations should in all likelihood be scrutinized and the prospects for tightening performance standards be considered. It may be that wage and salary structures are encumbered by gross inequities or that average compensation rates are gradually creeping above the going market scales—or perhaps the reverse is true and the quality of the workforce is, in consequence, progressively deteriorating. A reactivated job-evaluation program and detailed study aimed at rationalizing the wage and salary structure probably are needed.

In still another common occurrence, the budget contemplates an overhead cost structure contributing to breakeven points which are much too high to be tolerated with projected sales volumes. It is one of those myths that are never quite laid to rest that plant overhead is rigidly fixed and thus not much subject to adjustment. In actual truth, overhead as well as direct costs can and must be controlled within sufficiently broad limits. It merely takes more specific planning—more determined action. Onerous breakeven points which bear heavily upon high-overhead industries have been lowered often enough to prove conclusively that they can be remedied. The danger is that no one will become sufficiently exercised until volume declines and much of the damage has been done. The budget which displays the symptoms of excess overhead should quickly call into action a vigorous cost reduction program.

These illustrations, selected almost at random, serve to emphasize the basic fact underlying all efforts of executives to control events. Operating controls eventually are translated into cost controls. The system of control is dependent upon a performance budget, which in turn is linked inextricably with the system of accounts. And accounting records, if they are to be worth their salt, must relate operating actualities to predetermined expectations.

The Controller's Function

Executive responsibility for coordinating plans and creating the accounting mechanisms by which results are communicated and reconciled with plans is appropriately assigned in corporate affairs to the controller. His administrative functions represent the very heart of the system of managerial accounting and control.

There are always operating executives who mistrust the controller's motives, or what is deemed to be his tendency to over-systematize record-keeping activities. Possibly the critics feel that they are being placed on the defensive by this penchant for system. Sometimes, too, their uneasiness rises out of a lack of managerial sophistication; they are accustomed by previous habit to the informalities of visual and intensely personal controls which serve well enough in small enterprises. Executives poorly equipped for the heavy responsibilities they bear are often inclined to view the growth of system with acute discomfort. They are disposed to identify it as a source of unjustified additions to overhead with which they themselves may eventually be charged. They fear the rigidities and regimented group action to which system inevitably contributes.

Often such arguments are found on analysis to be colored somewhat by the advocates' own self-interest, but system should indeed never be encouraged for the sake of system. An indispensable element of flexibility must be preserved. Ample opportunity for dealing simply and directly always must be kept open when exceptions to the general rule are clearly dictated by common sense. Rigid rules applied with no proper sense of perspective have a way of soon acquiring unwarranted sanctity.

But system, like formalized structure in organization, is a

necessary counterpart and accompaniment of large-scale enterprise. Both bring a sense of order to the processes of management. Deprive executives of system and acute awareness of structural relationships, and their role soon degenerates into one of running frantically from place to place, figuratively putting out minor fires which adequate systems would have prevented in the first place.

VIII

The Motivation of Executives

THE PERFORMANCE OF BUSINESS EXECUTIVES, LIKE THAT OF EVERYONE else, frequently falls short of their full capabilities. But executive competence, though often in short supply, is by no means unattainable. There are accepted ways by which candidates with exceptional potential can be discovered, selected, and put to work. And the means by which their talents can subsequently be tested and refined through coaching and experience also are fairly well understood.

But while executive competence is essential for business success, something more is required. Executives must be *willing* to do their best. Personal skills are clearly of little value unless those possessing them can be induced to apply them to the job of working well together.

Alfred P. Sloan, Jr., in analyzing his career at General Motors, has said: "The causes of success or failure are deep and complex, and chance plays a part. Experience has convinced me, however, that for those who are responsible for a business, two important factors are motivation and opportunity." [1]

Opportunity itself is, of course, one of the most powerful motivating factors in human behavior. Men of competence, above all, want outlets for their talents. The spark of personal enthusiasm will soon be quenched unless executives in training

[1] Sloan, Alfred P., Jr., *My Years with General Motors,* Doubleday & Co., Inc., 1964, p. 429.

are permitted to exercise initiative and are given authority and responsibility for decisions commensurate with their capabilities. Organizations unable to change with changing conditions quickly become fertile executive recruiting grounds for their more aggressive and resourceful competitors.

Human Motives Extremely Diverse

Executive motivation in business enterprises is invariably contingent in some part upon financial inducement, though just what combination will trigger the desired reaction is always puzzling. The motives which stimulate individuals to do their best are personal and highly subjective. What any man's response will be at any given time or place depends upon his own special conditioning and background. His actions reflect what he himself has come to consider most important. So often, in the end, incentives are determined less by what is received than by the spirit in which it is offered.

The exact reasons why civilized men everywhere throw themselves unreservedly into cooperative efforts of their own choosing are almost as varied as human emotions. We need not suppose that business leaders are exceptions or that their social contribution is inferior because they are preoccupied with the economic affairs of life.

It is mankind's perpetual good fortune that there are in all well-ordered societies, in every generation and in diverse occupations, men and women who require no outside urging, who have within themselves all the incentive needed to do their best. They sometimes seem, in fact, almost totally indifferent to the prospect or lack of financial reward. This distinguished company unquestionably includes many very special talents: artists and poets struggling to give form to the beauties and spiritual yearnings which stir men's minds; philosophers and scientists burning with intellectual curiosity; humanists and healers absorbed in bettering life for those less fortunate than the rest; inventors, builders, and administrators bent on creating a more satisfying physical world; patriots and crusaders dedicated to freedom and human dignity.

The motives of all who are touched with genius clearly run the whole gamut of human emotions, from the purely selfish to the sublime. They may seem driven by a worldly urge for personal power; by a craving for commendation; by a stubborn spirit of craftsmanship; by the simple thrill of racing and joy in living; by a dedicated search for truth; by loyalty to family and respect for humankind; by an inborn sense of destiny; by love of justice or reverence for God. Whatever the motivating force may be, it is assurance enough that "man lives not by bread alone." But we cannot conclude—even in the case of potential saints and heroes—that men are ever totally indifferent to the supply of bread. There is, in fact, an equally pointed Scriptural reminder that men are "worthy of their hire."

Individuals are judged by the professions and the institutions with which they choose to identify themselves. Professed moralists, for example, are naturally expected to subscribe to some altruistic code. It probably would surprise no one for neighbors to express some doubts about a clergyman's dedication if he favored, to the exclusion of all others, the parish prepared to pay him most. Any hospital staff, to cite still another instance, would be resentful if its management showed cynical disrespect for the physician's oath of dedication to the healing arts. Similarly, academicians and scholars lay great stress upon freedom of inquiry. Research scientists are especially attracted by facilities and working surroundings which will promote their investigations. The military high command could hardly be elated if defense budgets were ever to be substantially reduced. And business executives would be thought particularly unworldly if they were to show complete indifference to sharing personally in the wealth which they themselves have helped to create.

Inducements in any field which fail to recognize and cultivate these special self-interests and motives will certainly miss the point. The emphasis in this discussion upon economic motives does not imply that executives are more impervious than other men to the intangible rewards which make life worth living. It is merely that business is concerned primarily with the economic sphere.

Requisites of an Effective Compensation Plan

The means by which management attempts to realize an effective compensation program for corporate executives are gradually becoming standard practice. Three basic objectives, however, need emphasis:

1. A base pay structure consistent with going rates in the executive labor market.
2. An equitable system of special rewards for special performance.
3. Stimulation of a deep sense of personal identification with corporate welfare.

These three are separate though complementary goals. Each presents a special problem requiring solution. Each needs examination in this general order. For a sound executive bonus system necessarily depends first, upon an equitable structure of base salaries, and second, the ideal of a closely knit community of interest among executives in their relations with each other and with their company. This is clearly unrealizable unless there is an acceptable plan providing positive rewards for special performance.

The heart of the compensation system in a free labor market is therefore a base rate scale which makes it possible to conform with the salaries that comparable jobs command from other bidders for executive services. What is considered fair pay in the current market for reasonable, though not necessarily exceptional, performance is the minimum standard. If, for extended periods, the salaries that are offered fall much below this going scale, the result is almost sure to be a rising rate of executive turnover, unfortunately among those who can least easily be spared. Nothing leads more certainly to eventual deterioration in the executive labor force.

There are sometimes notable exceptions, to be sure. When corporate fortunes require it temporarily, management—second only to the owners—must always be expected to feel the pressure. Executives on such occasions often do accept, quite willingly, rates of compensation considerably below what they deserve. In fact, it should surprise no one in times of austerity if there is general insistence that each executive bear his share, impartially and proportionately, of the general sacrifice asked of the group.

The point is that men in authority are likely to rise readily enough to emergencies provided they know the general burden is fairly distributed. But the complete facts on what is being asked of them must be laid bare for all to see. Disappointment and suspicion quickly poison men's minds when they believe they are being victimized. These are times when faulty internal communication plays havoc with morale.

The Base Rate Structure

A base salary structure must be sufficiently flexible to permit recognition of significant job differences, but these differences must be *really* significant lest the classification process become vague and burdened with senseless requirements. Even though the standard salary range, expressed in dollars from the lowest to the highest, may be extremely broad, the entire group of executive personnel can usually be contained adequately within a structure which has relatively few classes. To carry the process further may merely result in setting up job categories and subcategories with no real meaning. Manifestly, there is no point in assuming a degree of precision within the classification process which cannot exist.

The general pattern of this base rate structure can readily be charted in a two-dimensional scale from which standard job rates for each job class can be projected. On the base line of this chart, all job classes included in the series are spaced at uniform intervals in ascending order from left to right. On the vertical ordinate, beginning at the point of origin, a scale of relative job importance is laid out tentatively at appropriate intervals in ascending order. (The intervals can subsequently be rated and assigned appropriate dollar values.) Against these two coordinates, all job classes in the series are plotted, thus establishing an assumed base salary curve with an upward skew from left to right.

It is commonly agreed that the shape and slope of a curve suitable for the classification of executive jobs may differ substantially from the wage curves best suited for classifying other occupational categories, such as monthly-paid clerical employees or hourly wage earners. All have similar objectives but require different approaches.

Job ratings in the shop, as ultimately determined, are almost sure to reflect the influence of hard collective bargaining tactics. Much as one might like to measure job content with engineering precision, in the end negotiation is likely to play an important part in grading jobs. The necessities of compromise usually result in numerous job classes separated from one another by uniform, limited increments—seldom, in fact, more than a few cents per hour.

Clerical occupations also can be fitted to an objective salary rate scale by a similar approach. The resulting structure probably will not require as many separate classes as are needed for hourly wage occupations, but both series can be joined in a single compensation scale arranged in arithmetic progression with the two parts represented by straight lines of uniform slope.

Executive jobs, especially in the higher echelons of the series, are much more subjective in content. Numerical techniques of measurement, such as point rating, which serve well for shop or clerical jobs are likely to be cumbersome in evaluating and classifying these higher positions. The permissible limits separating one class from another at executive levels become progressively less certain as one rises in the scale, and the resulting classification is very likely to become less precise.

This classification is ordinarily determined by a ranking technique which consists in arranging all jobs in the series in ascending order of importance. Sometimes this ranking of jobs is preceded by a rating in terms of assumed point values, but this hardly seems essential in classifying executive jobs. Point rating gives the appearance of greater precision; but it, like the ranking technique, in the final analysis depends upon judgment. Experience has shown that executive jobs can readily be classified by direct comparison, taking into account what each position may be realistically expected to command in the executive labor market.

Comparisons with what other organizations pay are bound to be uncertain. The executive labor market is never very well organized, and identical job titles in different contexts often have quite different meanings. Despite these differences, however, a fair approximation of prevailing salary ranges—at least for carefully selected key job titles—can quickly be established. The job rate for foremen, as an example, representing what is usually the lowest level in the supervisory scale, is reasonably uniform in any given locality; that is, over an extended period it tends to be stabilized throughout the industrial community at an easily determinable level. Good information concerning salary rates for positions higher in the management scale, even up to the level of chief executive, also is obtainable,[2] though some investigation may be required and the appropriate data, once developed, must be used with discretion. Nevertheless these data do provide general guidelines for an acceptable executive salary scale model which can be adapted to the needs of any given organization. The finished design, of course, is a task for experts who calibrate the vertical ordinate or standard salary scale of the structure.

Job Worths and Control Points

The number of classes required to provide an adequate base rate scale, including all jobs of executive grade, actually is not great; even in large organizations it rarely exceeds 20 or thereabouts. The midpoints of these several classes are arranged in conformity with a "curve of best fit" (usually parabolic in form), in geometric progression, and in ascending order. Appropriate percentage differentials between classes are fairly easy to determine—say, somewhere between 15 and 20 percent under usual circumstances. The midpoint values thus established are assumed to represent "job worths"; that is, the competitive market rates of the jobs subsequently to be assigned in the classification process to each specific class.

[2] Compilations of executive salary data published and kept up to date by the Executive Compensation Service of the American Management Association, for example, include returns on key occupations from as many as 4,000 companies identified in terms of industries and significant size groupings.

It is, of course, hardly to be supposed in a dynamic and extremely fluid executive organization that all the jobs assigned to a given class will carry compensation rates which correspond exactly to the predetermined job worth or midpoint of the class. Complete conformance is unlikely no matter how accurately the value scale reflects competitive salary rates or how meticulously the classification process has been performed. But it is not necessary that exact conformity exist. Realism requires, in any case, a considerable degree of flexibility within the structure.

This quality of flexibility can be provided by establishing guidelines which mark off the upper and lower ranges of each class. These lines should be related, in general, to the one drawn through the midpoints to represent the job worths of the several classes. They are related to it by a fixed percentage, plus or minus, of the midpoint values, identical in amount to the percentage differential between the midpoints of adjacent classes. Thus they gradually diverge from these midpoints the higher one rises in the scale.

The dollar ranges of the several classes in the series, as established by these upper and lower limits, usually overlap to some degree the limits set for adjacent classes. The mid or "control" points of these adjacent classes will be clearly differentiated; but borderline jobs, so called because they are priced considerably above or below the designated control point, may call for special attention. If the deviation of the actual rate from the standard rate in any given instance is extreme, it is clearly conceivable that the job in question might have been classified in either the one or the other immediately adjacent class. Which one will depend upon whether the deviation is above or below the standard rate of the class to which the job has been assigned.

These noncomforming jobs stand out as exceptions to be dealt with individually. When they fall completely outside the established class range to which they have been assigned, they are customarily called "red circle" rates; and, provided the classification process has been carefully performed, job rates so designated are more than likely to represent downright inequities which should be corrected at the earliest opportunity.

On the whole, however, the job structure thus conceived is a realistic frame of reference for all classified jobs. It is a most convenient tool for preventing compensation rates from getting progressively out of control. The base rate structure can, for example, be safely assumed to be under control if the average of the rates actually being paid for jobs in each class is in reasonable conformity with the standard rate for the class. Out-of-line individual rates will be readily detected, but the structure in general will still be consistent with competition provided the established standard rates conform with the current market.

Should the average of the actual job rates tend in time to deviate from the standard in either direction, the situation naturally calls for remedy. If the trend is upward, the correct inference is that either the established standard is falling behind the current market and should be revised, or else excessively liberal adjustments in individual rates are beginning to pull the class average above what the jobs are worth in the market.

It is to be expected that some superior incumbents should command more than the standard rate, but the majority in any given class can hardly be so superior that they all merit this preferred treatment. They cannot all be above average.

If, on the other hand, the average tends to fall below the control point, it is quite likely that the actual salary scale is less than that of prevailing competition. In this case, the quality of performance will soon decline as superior employees respond to better offers elsewhere. Indeed, top-level executives may regard turnover among these superior people as a barometer which tells them whether their salary rate scales are remaining competitive. Thus they can keep informed without becoming personally involved in individual rate adjustments about which they cannot possibly be as knowledgeable as those in lower echelons nearer the point of pressure.

Classification the Essential Element

The classification of executive occupations in relation to valid salary standards is the essential element in any effective system of base salary control. In this way all jobs are appropriately related to one another through systematic and exhaustive comparison.

This process of comparison and ranking involves specifically:

1. Identifying each job.
2. Describing its distinctive characteristics.
3. Determining its general orientation within the organization.
4. Establishing the particular authority relationships under which the incumbents operate, the intended scope of their activities, and the person to whom they are accountable.
5. Projecting natural lines of promotion *to* this specific job and *from* it, in turn, to higher echelons of the organizational structure.

These data comprise the major substance of an organizational manual. Their compilation is obviously an important staff assignment which should be carried out under a "director of salary administration" or the equivalent.

The ranking process by which all the jobs identified are assigned to classes in the completed salary structure is necessarily a joint endeavor. It can best be undertaken by ad hoc management committees whose members are selected because of their personal familiarity with the jobs being classified in the local situation. These committees should be expected to act under the salary administrator's guidance. Their conclusions should be subject to approval for interdivisional consistency by the chief executive, whose recommendations concerning the broad outlines, though not the details, of the program might in turn be made to a permanent corporate committee on executive compensation above the temptations of personal involvement. The responsibilities of final review and approval that normally would be vested in this standing committee are clearly of sufficient urgency to warrant its being answerable directly to the board of directors and, in fact, to merit the more than casual attention of the board itself as the deliberative body of highest authority in the corporate organization. Scarcely anything exceeds in importance the means which stimulate executives to do their best.

Corporate managements unaccustomed to the disciplined control of executive payrolls sometimes are irked by the prospect of introducing what seem to be unduly elaborate procedures to this end. They may prefer to deal with such personal problems as the compensation of their immediate staffs on a less systematic and sometimes, indeed, a completely opportunistic basis. But system is one of the penalties of organizational growth. If the need for system is ignored and its introduction postponed too long, the inevitable result is haphazard administration and confusion. Executive compensation cannot be dealt with casually.

Special Effort Requires Special Incentive

Compensation rates which are both competitive and equitable are essential to maintaining morale and loyalty at all levels of employment. But, for executives at least, to be loyal employees is not enough. Because they must be stimulated to do more than just an adequate job, they must feel that special effort will be systematically recognized and rewarded.

Executives need this assurance more than any other employees. Theirs is invariably a group endeavor in which they are entrusted with real policy-making powers. They are continually haunted by disturbing doubts as to just how their individual involvement in these joint plans and stratagems will actually turn out. If the results are good, they may indeed find themselves acclaimed beyond their just deserts. But, if the results instead are bad, it is just as likely that they will be charged with shortcomings not completely under their own control. Each can be assured only that sooner or later his decisions will come home to roost and that, in making them, he is always exposed to grave personal risk. So who knows but that, if nothing is ventured, his timidity will go unnoticed?

A straight salary system alone, no matter how liberal, rarely creates the climate which encourages positive and courageous executive action when *no* action may often seem the safer course. There is, after all, no very good reason why executives—highly paid but with no quickening sense of proprietorship—should strive harder, take longer personal risks, in the hope of earning still further salary increases which, in these modern days, will for the most part be claimed by the tax collector.

It is obviously to the advantage of both executives and their employers to be placed in "the position they would occupy if they were conducting the business on their own account." [3] As corporations grow and executives tend to lose this heartwarming feeling of partnership in the business, the most powerful incentive attributable to private enterprise may all but disappear. It is indeed a perilous stage in any organized effort when participants begin to think of their relation to it in terms of a vague and impersonal "they" instead of a distinctly personal "we."

One of the chief bulwarks of the private enterprise system is the fact that the privileges and responsibilities of property ownership provide powerful incentives to be prudent and diligent in business. No one in his right mind will deliberately waste his own resources or, through neglect and indifference, permit his own position to be undermined in competition.

These satisfactions of proprietorship constitute the lure which induces many of the more venturesome and self-reliant candidates entering business each year to try it on their own account. If they fail, it is much more likely to be from lack of competence or experience than from lack of effort and attention. True, some will subsequently give up or lose control when the business grows and they fail to grow with it. Many men who do quite well as sole proprietors in modest surroundings find the ordeal beyond them when, in search of greater capital, the business "goes public" and they become only one of many stockholders instead.

Executives have no difficulty in maintaining a strong sense of personal responsibility toward anything they own. But this attitude inevitably undergoes subtle changes—which even they may recognize only dimly—when they are placed in circumstances in which they no longer have a strong proprietorship interest. This change in executive attitudes, which quite frequently has serious consequences, is not uncommon in large-scale enterprise—whether private or governmental. Men under direct administrative obligations in either environment tend to become less and less personally involved with the owners or the electorate from whom their mandate is derived. Nor is their sense of personal responsibility likely to be sharpened when the transactions

[3] Alfred P. Sloan, Jr., places great emphasis on this belief as a cardinal element in corporate success. *Op. cit.*, pp. 407–419.

in which they play a part assume magnitudes which clearly strain mortal comprehension.

What credence can be given, for example, to assertions even upon the highest executive authority that a national budget of $100 billion is "tight"? Who can really tell with any assurance the order of priority or degree of essentiality which should be accorded to the individual items, almost beyond number, which compose it? Who is competent to insist, in the political effort to annihilate opposition before it gets organized, that proposals to reduce this budget by so much as a fragment are clearly irresponsible? Can anyone in authority possibly know how much discrepancy between outgo and income, as expressed in billions, can be tolerated—and for how long—before it jeopardizes the national welfare?

Or, in the much narrower confines of corporate business, what within reason constitutes an adequate appropriation for new long-term capital expenditures in a $5- or $10-billion firm? How many millions ought to be spent on research, none of which may be reflected in corporate earnings for months—perhaps even years—to come?

How can imponderables of such astronomical proportions be documented and convincingly supported by quantitative proof? It truly is extraordinary to expect that administrators charged with spending "other people's money" in these dimensions will apply the same standards of prudence, will display the same solicitude for efficiency, will experience the same torment of indecision with which competent executives approach similar, though less momentous, problems in the management of their own affairs. Obviously, a healthy and continuing sense of proprietorship, provided it can be created and preserved, is the most powerful executive motivation that can be devised.

The Basic Motivational Factors

The basic motivations to which all employees—including wage earners, nonsupervisory salaried workers, and executives—respond differ not so much because different people have different urges as because of their different relations to the organization and their quite different obligations to it.

Wage earners and salaried clerical and technical workers obviously are no more and no less interested than managers, per se, in making more money for other people. They ordinarily have no personal contacts with the owners and are not likely to be greatly interested in whether a profit is made or not. They may even feel little enthusiasm about opportunities to improve operating efficiency in their own departments, especially should these be related in their minds to the possibility of working themselves out of a job.

Their collective understanding of their personal involvement in the process of corporate profit making is slight. That their own behavior may increase or lessen the hazard of incurring a loss is not of much lasting concern to them. They personally assume no great sense of responsibility for profits and feel no remorse should losses occur. If they were to be offered the chance to share in profits, especially if it implied loss sharing as well, the proposal could readily cause suspicion rather than provide incentive.

The real factors which elicit willingness to cooperate in the joint endeavor at these nonexecutive levels, especially among collective bargaining groups, are about as follows:

1. Take-home income—often, in fact, with no very significant distinction among base pay, performance bonuses, and fringe benefits.
2. Assurance of job security and uninterrupted employment.
3. Assurance of sympathetic understanding and personal advancement to better-paying or socially preferable jobs.

For executives—with their closer contacts with the owners, their better understanding of the nature of profit, and their greater ability to influence company policy and profitability—these several factors assume some such order of importance as this:

1. Base income.
2. Status.
3. Special recognition in the form of bonuses for special

achievement contributing more or less directly to corporate welfare.

4. Opportunity to participate personally in company growth and enrichment—doubtless of rapidly increasing importance with progressive improvements in personal status relative to one's associates in management.

The first two of these factors are mainly provided for through a well-administered base salary structure. A stimulating and successful management group, good leadership, and an enlightened and constructive promotion policy are important supplements. Periodic increases in base salary in recognition of improved personal performance or in connection with increased authority and responsibility amply satisfy personal cravings for status, especially if they keep pace with the recipient's personal spending habits.

The third factor—special rewards for special performance—is the basic justification for executive bonus plans. The fourth—encouragement of the proprietary interests of executives—is the underlying purpose of stock ownership plans. Clearly, neither is adequately provided for under modern conditions by base salary provisions alone, however liberal.

It is impractical to reward executives adequately for exceptional but isolated achievements by raising their base salaries. If persisted in, this will eventually distort the whole salary structure, and special cash payments in any case lose their glamour when taxed away. A salary increase that is not occasioned by promotion but, instead, is intended as a reward for some special and possibly nonrecurring service inevitably creates an indefinite commitment. It is no more logical, in fact, than the disproportionate increase in an executive's bonus allotment which not infrequently is granted in recompense for failure to adjust a base rate which, unhappily, has fallen behind the going market rate.

Special bonus rewards for special services permit executives to break out of the salary schedule without permanently upsetting it. If, in addition, they are related to stock acquisition, they contribute to managerial stability by building up a vested interest which becomes more and more valuable in time.

This is not the place to set forth the precise specifications of an ideal executive bonus and stock acquisition plan. Needs differ from company to company just as they do for different grades of employment within the same company. Incentive systems, whether for executives or nonexecutives, ought to be tailored to the local scene. There are, nevertheless, certain generalizations which experience seems to suggest are of well-nigh universal application—regardless, in some cases, of the specific occupational grades included in the program.

1. *Bonus plans are intended to stimulate participants to superior performance.* This is their unique purpose wherever used in the organization—from wage earners in the shop to top-echelon executives. The underlying logic was never more tersely stated than by Frederick W. Taylor almost 75 years ago when he observed that men will not do an extraordinary day's work for an ordinary day's pay.

Employee compensation at all levels of employment has traditionally been determined in terms either of performance or of time on the job. In the shop, wages have been quoted at so much per piece or so much per hour. Modern practice has, however, tended increasingly to base pay upon some combination of significant factors, including personal output, time spent, and general status accorded the job. The resulting innovations have assumed numerous forms, from variations of so-called "measured day work" to plans for a time wage supplemented by additional payments for accomplishment in excess of a predetermined standard.

These developments in compensation practice in the plant, combining base pay and special incentives, provide the pattern for all modern bonus plans. The methods of computation used and the specific factors to be considered differ from handyman to general manager, but the theory is always the same. The objective is to stimulate and hold men to high-level performance, though it is a mistake to assume that any system of payment can ever, by itself, take the place of disciplined supervision.

2. *Bonus plans, to be acceptable, must be an integral part of the compensation program.* The ancient custom—perhaps most firmly grounded in military tradition—of special citations, decorations, and awards for services "beyond the usual call of duty"

no doubt has its value. The ceremonial occasions on which such awards are made may even serve a useful purpose in business; formal suggestion systems with provision for public recognition, for instance, sometimes are of great value if well administered. But incentive programs, for maximum effect, must be consistently maintained. Bonuses which are given so rarely and so unexpectedly as to seem capricious to the surprised recipients probably have little sustained incentive value.

It is not always feasible, obviously, to compute and distribute bonuses as frequently as base salary payments, though they should not be postponed so long as to deprive the bonus program of standard-practice status. Partial payments on a quarterly or biannual basis, or immediately after the conventional year-end reckoning, clearly work no hardship upon high-level executives. Hourly workers naturally expect much more frequent accounting.

3. *Bonus payments should always be dependent upon factors which eligible participants are in a position to influence by their own performance.* This direct cause-and-effect relationship is indispensable. It is the essential which most often distinguishes executive bonuses from the general "bonuses," so called, which are sometimes distributed almost promiscuously to employees of lesser rank.

Executive bonuses have a natural, direct relationship with the total profit-making potential of the corporate organization or division. Executives are distinguished from all other employee groups by their personal possession of policy-determining powers which, as we have seen, make it possible for them to influence corporate profit performance directly. They are charged, as is no one else, with final accountability for the broad composite of operations—for customer satisfaction, for effective control of capital, for sound management of inventories and receivables, for operating efficiencies, for competitive position and market coverage. No single index reflects management's success or failure in bringing this huge and intricate complex of activities under control quite so graphically as the rate of return on capital investment. Executive bonuses, in consequence, are almost always made contingent upon profit performance.

By this test, eligibility for participation is quite properly exclusive. Real responsibility for corporate or divisional profits, even in the best possible pattern of decentralized authority, is necessarily confined to top-level corporate and divisional executives comprising a relatively small proportion of the total supervisory group. As a practical matter, the cut-off point usually can be fairly fixed at some appropriate minimum base salary or organizational level.

This exclusiveness can itself be of incentive value. Within the group of participants so fortunate as to qualify, this distinguishing mark of status is calculated to create a tremendously effective driving force. And upon those in junior positions, not yet eligible but with hope and potential for becoming eligible, this powerful, intangible incentive is by no means lost—provided, once again, the plan is wisely administered.

There is often a temptation to enlarge the boundaries of eligibility for bonus participation beyond the point of real significance. This is a mistake. For, if made universal, participation ceases to be a special distinction and quickly becomes instead a vested interest for everyone.

Profit sharing, for example, seems in some quarters on the way to becoming a magic word—supposedly providing a remedy for almost all the troublesome tensions in employer-employee relations. The concept has, indeed, great emotional appeal. Employees at all levels are easily attracted by it. Labor's representatives can enthusiastically approve it as increasing the fringe benefits of their constituents. Critics of private capitalism with little real understanding of how it works can readily become sympathetic advocates of general profit sharing by all employees. They eagerly endorse splitting up what they assume to be a sort of unearned increment accruing, for the most part, to absentee owners and, in their own prejudiced estimation, much too large in any event.

Actually, the term "profit sharing" in this supposedly attractive context is little more than muddled semantics devoid of meaning. "Profit," in the accountant's specialized vocabulary, is *return to owners* in recompense for contributing capital and —let it never be forgotten—underwriting losses should they occur. Profit and loss are inseparably linked in this calculation: To speak of profit sharing by employees, with no obligations respecting losses, has no more meaning in any technical sense than would "wage sharing" by owners or sharing by either owners or wage earners in collections from accounts receivable.

Executive bonuses, though properly contingent upon profits —or, preferably, the rate of return on investment—are by the same token never (strictly speaking) profit-sharing plans. Indeed, if they are soundly designed and administered, their promised payments do not diminish but rather enhance the net return on investment. Really good bonus plans, no matter how liberal, never work hardship upon owners.

4. *The heart of an executive bonus system lies in its effect on the individual recipient.* A dynamic merit-rating procedure is indispensable if there is to be an impartial and knowledgeable determination of individual awards.

The total executive bonus pool each year, if contingent upon some predetermined relationship with the current rate of return on investment, can readily be established by formula. But to introduce a conditional provision at this crucial point does add flexibility. The chief executive and the board of directors should reserve the opportunity to adjust the overall dimensions of bonus distributions. This indubitable right of the final corporate authority to use discretion and judgment in what it deems to be the corporate interest ought never to be completely relinquished— no more for bonuses than for dividends.

Once the pool is established, it must be broken down into the various segments of operations which call for separate treatment—a problem quite properly disposed of by formula—and finally allotted to individual participants. Opinions may differ widely as to whether divisional executive bonus allotments should be contingent upon their own division's performance only; upon some combination of divisional and corporate performance; or upon overall corporate performance only. To base divisional bonuses exclusively on the division's own performance unquestionably keys the reward to the specific factors over which local executives have most control. But, on the other hand, it encourages parochial thinking—which often needs no special encouragement.

Some divisions, by nature, are inherently more profitable than others, and the differences are not always of the respective managements' own making. It is doubtless desirable to focus each participant's efforts upon those responsibilities for which he is personally charged, but not at the risk of his losing sight of the overriding interest of the corporation as a whole. Divisional executives, like all others, are in final terms corporate executives as well.

These different points of view on the design of the bonus system all have their staunch adherents. There are many precedents in practice for each position; and whichever choice is made is likely to be based, not on theory, but on local traditions and experience. Of much more pertinence to the individual participant, in any case, is how his own share is determined.

Ideally, each executive's sharing in the bonus pool should be discretionary. It should be determined by his superior after careful appraisal of what specific contribution to the common effort he has made. But, alas, the extreme difficulty of making accurate judgments about individual performance—and the difficulty increases rapidly as organizations grow and become less personal—makes it well-nigh impossible for the top echelons either to find the time or have the first-hand knowledge to exercise the degree of discretion which they, in good conscience, would like. When communication breaks down, discretionary decisions unfortunately tend more and more to be decided by formula, simply because those with power to make the decisions lack sufficiently precise knowledge to exercise the discretion.[4]

The byproducts of the important ritual of periodically distributing the bonus sometimes are among its greatest values. The occasion provides, for one thing, the best possible opportunity for supervisors to engage subordinates in man-to-man discussion of their relative strengths and weaknesses. Frank criticism is an indispensable part of every executive development program—else how can anyone be expected to correct his mistakes and make progess? But, if there seldom is any time when it is more important for all those in authority to join their subor-

---

[4] Sometimes a compromise seems best. A fixed percentage is reserved for discretionary awards to those deemed especially worthy. The major portion of the pool is then distributed in proportion to the respective base salaries of the participants—a specially impelling reason for first making sure that base salaries are equitable.

dinates in natural and frankly personal appraisal, there is none when many executives will be less inclined to do so. And yet, to the anxious and quite possibly resentful subordinate, what can be more crucial, when plagued with growing fears of disfavor, than to know where he stands and why?

Perhaps the mutual embarrassment which this obligation often generates results from the fact that neither the appraiser nor the one appraised can ever be completely sure that his personal judgment is correct. But it is an obligation which always accompanies the exercise of authority. When resolutely and fairly faced, it can cement relations at their very best between teacher and student, between coach and trainee, between supervisor and supervised.

5. *Bonus compensation is intended to represent the "extra margin" in the participant's income.* From the corporate point of view, it would be distinctly desirable if these special payments to executives were normally reserved by the recipients for systematic savings, investment, and—especially—progressive build-up of an ownership position in the company. As a matter of fact, prior to the high-tax era beginning approximately at the time of World War II, executive bonuses were, in some notable instances, paid altogether in company stock as an incentive to extraordinary effort.

Steeply progressive income taxes bear with special severity upon executives whose major sources of income have no ready means of escape. These modern burdens have made what would otherwise be a logical practice largely impractical for two reasons: Cash payments have become necessary to permit the payment of current taxes; and stock option plans have become popular as a way of creating capital gains, thus substituting for currently "constructive receipt."

Congressmen may deplore stock option practices and strive to eliminate them as "tax loopholes." But this does not get at the root of the matter. Tax laws always encourage resourceful victims to seek escape. It is estimated that approximately two-thirds of all the companies listed on the New York Stock Exchange use stock option plans, though it doubtless would be extremely difficult indeed to determine how many of these plans were established in the first place merely as devices for tax relief and how many for the much more constructive purpose of encouraging those eligible for executive bonuses to become corporate stockholders.

It has often been assumed that executives coming under stock option plans quickly divest themselves of ownership as soon as they become eligible for claiming substantial capital gains. This, if true, is deplorable, but the situation would seem to be considerably exaggerated; recent surveys appear to indicate that possibly as much as 70 percent of executive stock option stock is retained by the purchasers beyond the period necessary to establish significant tax advantages.

It is quite unlikely, perhaps, that in most large enterprises the entire executive group will ever again—individually or collectively—become major stockholders. It is much more important from the corporate point of view that their stock holdings comprise the major part of their own private fortunes. Their personal success must somehow be made to depend upon corporate success. Clearly, the most constructive and powerful motivating force that can be devised for corporate executives is attitudes that will impel them to conduct the business as if it were their very own.

IX

The Quest for Permanence

IT APPARENTLY IS THE ALMOST UNIVERSAL DESIRE OF ALL INSTITUTIONS, whatever their functions may be, to achieve permanence. No progressive business management is ever indifferent to this absorbing quest. It is an urge which affects all alike, regardless of size, from the one-man shop at the one extreme to General Motors at the other. Seldom is an enterprise so small, in fact, or its founder so devoid of imagination that he does not sometimes indulge in dreams of projecting his creation beyond his own lifetime.

Many of today's largest business organizations trace their growth to modest beginnings and personal ambitions. Their present managements, though their power has multiplied manyfold, must still be alert, no less than their hardy predecessors, to the problems of survival. Indeed, despite their enormously increased resources, the prospect of *not* surviving may seem at times more imminent now than ever.

Small businesses, unhampered by burdensome overhead, sometimes seem capable of concentrating, if they will, upon special service to their customers. Large businesses also must win customer approval; but special and individualized service is likely to play havoc with customary routines. Increased importance always brings new obligations, magnifies overhead, and creates new contingencies. Because of their new status, managements must accept, in greatly increased measure, distracting commitments as responsible members of the community.

Two major conditions of survival confront private institutions—the one traceable to external and the other to internal origins:

1. All are obligated to gain public acceptance as institutions deserving to continue.
2. Permanence in any institution depends, also, upon the resourcefulness of its own leadership in contriving internal stability.

Public Acceptance of Private Business

The dependence of private business upon public sanctions is one of the common facts of economic life. Corporate businesses owe their existence to charter by the state. Service businesses usually operate under license and thus are constantly exposed to regulation. Big businesses, because of their very size, are particularly vulnerable to public criticism. Small businesses, because they are small, are the subjects of special governmental solicitude—and understandably so, first because they suffer from devastating mortality rates and, second, because a healthy competitive system is dependent upon large numbers of effective competitors.

It is a continuing obligation of government, in a society which permits and depends upon private enterprise, to exercise its police powers in the regulation of business with forbearance. Society's first concern is to preserve the values inherent in this system and to avoid setting in motion or permitting to be set in motion forces that will lead to its gradual destruction. Private business, obviously, is similarly obligated. Sound relationships between business and government in fulfillment of this joint commitment clearly take precedence over even the relations between a business and its customers as the basic condition for survival.

It is natural that spokesmen for business should develop selfish points of view. They are certain to resist what they consider to be unwarranted encroachments of public policy upon their own special domain. And, when some arm of government makes demands upon private business interests that are inconsistent with their right to continue, these private agencies, through their spokesmen, must protest as convincingly as they are able.

It is equally to be expected that politically oriented representatives of government—no less self-centered, no less subject to partisan jealousies—need constant reminders that our system is a system of laws, not persons, and that this imposes just as great an obligation to avoid senseless harassment of the innocent (even though they may be large and powerful corporations) as to restrain the guilty.

Neither businessmen nor politicians can afford to be eternally critical of one another. They must join forces. They are equally obligated to develop ideas and to establish rules defining the correct relationships between government and business.

Proposals, no matter where they come from, must be stubbornly resisted if they will affect adversely the willingness of men to make new investments; if they will gradually undermine the profit base of industry and thus retard growth; if they will discourage efforts to maintain high levels of employment; if they will favor one pressure group to the detriment of other, equally deserving groups. Such resistance is in no sense obstructionism, for, should unwise counsels prevail, they will eventually bring disaster to corporate interests and to public interests as well.

It is obvious, nevertheless, that private managements should never be permitted to dictate the explicit conditions upon which public acceptance is to be granted. It is enough that they be able to exert their best influence. Like all articulate members of a free society, business executives certainly have the right and duty to use every legitimate means of persuasion at their disposal to influence public policy in their favor. This climate should be congenial to business. But, when business interests succeed in dominating public policy, the danger line has been crossed. Who knows when this overpowering influence will begin to injure other private interests that are quite as beneficent?

There is a single tenable position for private managements to assume. They must set a course conforming with the requirements of public policy, as it evolves in response to valid contentions from all sides, and hope that this course will prove rewarding.

Internal Stability and Sound Organization

The second major condition of survival, as already suggested, is greatly complicated by the fact that, although institutions may aspire to something akin to permanence, these aspirations are dependent upon persons with very limited tenure. Executives, no matter how essential their presence at any given moment may seem, actually exert an influence which at best is short-lived. Once they are unavailable, it is almost certain that they will not be long remembered. The cooperative effort, in any case, must continue in the hands of their successors. To insure continuance, those who are temporarily in control must therefore possess sure instincts for recognizing and accommodating change. They must also be capable of discovering, attracting, nurturing, testing, disciplining, and motivating competent replacements.

Like all structures, organizations must be soundly planned and built if they are to endure. It is a curious fact, nevertheless, that many managements appear to be primarily concerned with their investments in brick and mortar, which, though public monuments to success, soon become obsolete and often are torn down in less than a generation. These material investments seem actually to take precedence in managerial thinking over the renewal of their human resources. It is a common failing to be more interested in machines which, should they be destroyed, can readily be replaced than in men who must be depended upon to provide the sort of effective and self-renewing organization which is inevitably the work of years. As Clarence B. Randall has observed, "we have done far better with machines than with men."[1] Yet the men we pick or advance are a far better index of managerial ability than the plants that we build and the equipment we fill them with.

Constructive organization planning of any sort is based first of all upon determining what resources are already available. This inventory of executive manpower should aim at uncovering precisely where men of potential are located within the organi-

[1] Randall, Clarence B., *A Creed for Free Enterprise,* Atlantic—Little, Brown and Company, 1952, p. 52.

zation; how well their latent talents are being developed; what preparations they themselves are making toward future growth and enhanced usefulness; and when they will be ready for increased responsibilities.

The object of this search is to insure that there is strength in depth supporting all critical decision centers throughout the structure. One of the most disconcerting questions which can be asked of many executives is, "Who will be ready to take your place when you are no longer available?"

Age and tenure represent essential criteria, but sometimes by no means the most important ones, for determining the suitability of executive incumbents for advancement. These factors do possess great finality, of course, and are readily predictable since no one seems ever to succeed for long in postponing the ravages of age. It can be most revealing, in fact, to record and compare the ages of present incumbents at successive levels within the organization structure. Probably the average age differential between executive levels should ideally never be less than five years, and possibly it should never be much more than ten in a well-kept organization.

An organization structure ought always to be capable of renewal, for the most part, by orderly progression from within. Vice presidents are the most likely recruiting ground for future chief executives. But this cannot be if all the vice presidents are already older than the president and approaching retirement. Department managers may be the natural material for future vice presidents. But, if so, the average age of the present incumbents at this level should be substantially less than the present average of vice presidents. In the same way, a shop in which the divisional superintendents are, on the average, appreciably younger than their corresponding assistant superintendents, and in which the foremen have grown old in service, may be currently capable of first-rate performance. But it is bound to have trouble eventually in finding well-trained supervisory replacements unless something is done to reverse this trend.

Inversion of the age progression through the various levels of an organization usually indicates that management either has failed to recruit capable supervisors at lower levels or else has been unable to provide sufficiently attractive opportunities for advancement from these levels to hold those people who are most capable of growth. Provision of such opportunities for men of good potential in the lower ranks of management is, in fact, the chief reason why company growth is considered by farsighted executives to be so important.

The planning of an organization, like that of any structure, is greatly assisted by careful analysis. Executives are frequently amazed when first confronted with an accurate organization chart of the activities for which they are responsible. They may have been vaguely aware, to be sure, that their organization was defective, but they are unable to see just why this was so until the authority relationships have been plotted and job descriptions have been reduced to written forms.

The conventional organization chart helps materially to portray these relationships, in their strengths and weaknesses, as they exist at a given moment. Its chief value doubtless results from the disciplined thinking about organization which is required of everyone who undertakes to prepare such a chart and submit it periodically to rigorous review—a process which actually should include three portrayals instead of one:

1. The chart of organization as it currently exists, usually influenced strongly by improvised adaptations to the strengths and weaknesses, the peculiar quirks and particular achievements of present executive incumbents.
2. A supplementary portrayal reflecting what would seem to be a logical arrangement if these factors representing executive shortcomings and vested interests could be disregarded.
3. Still a third portrayal—of top-drawer significance to all chief executives—identifying potential executive talent seeded at various locations within the present structure.

Organizational arrangements always are influenced by adaptations to personal factors, but these should be adaptations to the strengths and weakness of *incumbents*. As occasions are afforded by replacements, activities ought to be regrouped in conformity, to the extent practicable, with the ideal. (Of course it may be necessary to adapt to inherent characteristics of the new executives.) These are the times when needed structural changes can be made with the least confusion. Unless critical faults have been identified and plans laid for their correction in advance, and in an atmosphere of relative detachment, the evolving structure is almost sure to be affected by severe pressures as vacancies occur unexpectedly and replacements must be made with insufficient thought. Under these circumstances the structure is bound to become gradually less rational in concept, less adapted to changing requirements, till, eventually, a revolutionary structural overhauling becomes essential.

But assistance in the onerous responsibility of identifying potential executive talents within the present workforce is clearly the central aim of all systematic organization planning. No other type of executive decision is likely to be as impelling and baffling as that pertaining to the selection of subordinate personnel for greater responsibilities. Decisions of this sort require deliberate and anxious attention. They must be jealously held as "strictly classified information" until announced. They ought always to be based squarely upon systematic and objective appraisals of the performance of every possible candidate in every related position of key responsibility.

Every chief executive, if he is to make these decisions with assurance, must know the answers to many troublesome questions about his subordinate executives, not merely indulge in wishful thinking about them. What specifically, for instance, are the shortcomings of present incumbents in key jobs? (These key jobs may be so numerous that personal acquaintance by the chief executive is totally impractical.) What precisely is needed to correct these shortcomings? When will replacement become necessary? Which candidates show the greatest promise of being eligible to fill vacancies when the choice can no longer be postponed? What should be done to hasten the development of potential candidates in anticipation of the eventual decision? All these questions must be analyzed, impersonally considered, and finally answered with as great detachment and wisdom as can be brought to bear on them. They ought never to be made impetuously after vacancies have already occurred and people's minds are filled with uncertainties and near-panic which must be quickly assuaged.

Solidarity of the Executive Group

The executive environment is one in which the personal associations of each man within his official sphere of influence ought to be quite intimate. But, in practice, the barriers with which men deliberately surround themselves tend to defeat this desirable goal. As organizations grow, each executive's circle of intimates rarely grows as rapidly as the managerial group as a whole. Everyone in authority is inevitably thrown into constant contact with his immediate superiors, those subordinates who report to him directly, and, of course, those occupying the same general level of authority as he does himself. Beyond this circle, distance and infrequent opportunity for face-to-face communication soon tend to make relative strangers of people—those above whose orders and instructions are awaited for guidance and those beneath, in the outposts of operations, who will be counted upon eventually to act upon these directives.

It is natural, unfortunately, that in this progressively less personal climate each individual executive may be motivated more and more by his own interests. *Esprit de corps* is a phenomenon most likely to occur in small and tightly knit groups; and, when this integrating influence is largely lacking, great persuasiveness is required to induce participants to accept the uncertain returns from cooperation in joint, large-scale activities without serious personal reservations. After all, no one member of the group can possibly control his own part in the cooperative effort to his exact liking. Loyalty is expected; and unqualified support of company objectives is insisted upon, even though these objectives may inspire, in many, little real enthusiasm.

As often as not, to remote rank-and-file participants and even to minor executives, this requirement of company allegiance is quite secondary to more personal loyalties. Why should unsparing devotion be expected of everyone when individual effort will most probably be subordinated beyond recognition to the combined efforts of the group? Why talk about team spirit when, to most, this will mean a self-effacing role, with assignments which appear quite inferior in comparison with those of more fortunate or more talented participants in their executive group?

The difficulty of securing willing response to the group's requirements is increased by the members' numerous affiliations with organizations beyond the jurisdiction of the firm. Conflicting loyalties to institutions of various sorts are, of course, a common personal experience in a free society. Individuals, whether executives or not, feel completely at liberty—at least outside regular working hours—to associate with whomever they choose in pursuit of mutually attractive goals. What an executive must especially avoid in these external relations is any serious conflict of interest which will impair his obligations to the firm. Each in his accustomed place must be depended upon to steer clear of embarrassing entanglements. To do so is a most important test of executive responsibility.

But the role of the executive's superiors in discouraging divided loyalties is unmistakable. Cooperative effort, if realized at all, must be stimulated by constant personal example from above. It is rare, indeed, that without this example the desired executive attitudes are spontaneously generated. Valid attitudes are instead most likely to be inspired and maintained by an insistent pressure based on discipline.

A healthy feeling of solidarity is without doubt an essential goal to which the full efforts of the organization must be directed. But how can we determine whether the most dedicated effort will realize this ultimate objective? What standards can be proposed for guidance in organization building? How may we be sure that the structure which appears to fit the firm's internal needs will, in turn, be consistent with the external setting of its operations?

Clearly, the structure best suited to a given situation is influenced by local conditions affecting the enterprise's particular social and economic environment. What must always be remembered is that the organization process is a means, never an end. There are no perfect structural designs which unmistakably represent the "good" organization; there are merely recognizable factors in human relationships, social conditions, resource availability, economic opportunities, competitive pressures, and public regulations which, in a given situation, suggest generalizations of apparent validity.

The Satisfaction of Rival Ends

There may be some guiding principles which have evolved out of long experience in attempting to reconcile this multitude of interdependent circumstances, and these principles doubtlessly do afford wise administrators some promise of success. The best organization structure is, in short, that structure which works best. But this question-begging conclusion depends inevitably upon the consideration of ends.

The trouble is that the ends of good organization are likely, at any one time, to depend upon whose interests momentarily seem most important. To some, wages and the personal satisfaction and security of wage earners are paramount; to others, opportunity to grow in executive stature; to still others, profits, consumer satisfaction, or the amount of tax revenue which can be exacted without jeopardizing future taxing potential.

The urge toward every one of these goals is clearly important in the quest for permanence. Without equitable and competitive wages, the capable seek other employment. Without opportunities for growth, employees with real potential are lost. Without profits, investors are reluctant to continue their support. Without products that have distinct market appeal, customers take their business elsewhere. Without a broad and fertile corporate tax base, present-day governmental revenue and functions would necessarily undergo drastic changes, with serious repercussions on the national economy.

Each firm's chances of survival depend upon reasonable satisfaction of all these rival demands. How to organize activities so as to maintain their varied pressures in approximate balance is an executive responsibility which never ends. The late John Dewey placed this unremitting task in proper perspective when he observed that "organizations have a continuing responsibility for conserving existing values so that those who come after may receive this heritage more solid and more secure, more widely accessible and more generously shared."

Failure to realize this high aim, should it occur in any particular firm, is inevitably an executive failure. It frequently is one of the hazards of an aging organization. Eventually it is the lot of

every executive to become less vigorous, less effective than perhaps he formerly was, at the very time when accumulating
vested interests and the sanctity of long service place a sort of
moratorium upon the insistence that he make way for a younger
man.

Protocol and good manners usually prevent subordinates
from making an issue of creeping inadequacies in executives
who outrank them, and those in higher authority who must act
to correct the situation often are unaware of the tensions which
are building up beneath.

The Penalties of Size

We have already observed that a breakdown in internal communication, even within the executive group itself, is an almost
inevitable concomitant of organizational growth. It should be
obvious, too, that this breakdown greatly increases the danger of
unrealistic decisions on matters vitally affecting the interests of
those far removed from the centers of authority. When this
occurs, conventions of more or less arbitrary application usually begin to be substituted for special judgments and decisions
fitted to individual cases.

There are many places where these easily recognized rigidities begin to make their appearance: unbending rules on executive retirement, for example; emphasis upon seniority as the
guiding factor in determining executive status, compensation
levels, promotions, or layoffs; special deference to rank; insistence in internal communication upon following explicitly the
prescribed channels of command. All are areas in which, traditionally, precedents quickly are established in large organizations. These may prove quite discouraging to young executives
in waiting; yet, when properly conceived, they can just as easily
open opportunities for promotion.

For, while overinsistence upon precedent is clear evidence of
growing bureaucracy, it is also true that bureaucracy is not altogether the unmixed curse it is sometimes represented to be. It
is, in some measure, an indispensable development in all large-
scale enterprises. Conventional practices may have good reason

for observance, even though they sometimes lead to quite unrealistic decisions and unfortunate actions and even though they
encourage automatic determinations in difficult cases which
might better be dealt with in terms of their own merits.

For instance, compulsory retirement at some arbitrarily
chosen age subjects everyone to uniform treatment. It sets a
definite date for one of the most emotion-burdened episodes in
the executive's organization experience. It removes the temptation to indulge in favoritism.

The chief objection to explicit retirement rules is that they
may not fit the individual case exactly. Some executives, unfortunately, for lack of early opportunity or because of personal
inhibitions, pass their peak and become likely prospects for de-
motion in middle life or not much later. Others continue to grow
in wisdom and potential usefulness long beyond the normal span
of executive service. To apply a single inexorable rule to them
all does help to clear administrative channels of those who
would prefer to linger on in authority in spite of declining
powers. But it does not retain for the organization those who
are still in full vigor despite their years, nor does it solve the
problem of correcting mistaken judgments respecting those who
have become prematurely ineffective.

Seniority—which of course is a matter of record—is a most
convenient criterion by which to justify administrative reluctance to deal forthrightly with flagrant inadequacies in executive circles. It is a factor which probably is given more weight
than it deserves in selecting candidates for promotion. It provides a clear-cut answer and saves executives the annoyance of
seeking more valid reasons for the choice which must be made.
But competent men who lack this credential through no fault of
their own may unfortunately be let go when others less worthy
are retained.

No administrator can be charged with partiality to his personal cronies if he insists on rigid application of the seniority
rule. The trouble is that seniority of itself never has much direct
bearing upon individual executive ability. It ordinarily is given
great weight in dealing with employee problems in collective
bargaining groups—probably with considerable justification.
Aside from considerations of health and serious lack of skills,

the range between man and man among those who work with their hands or tend machines is not often so great as to play havoc with efficiency. Some easily applied and objective criterion for selection is a welcome expedient.

The basis of preference in executive selection is—or should be—quite different. Seniority may be equated with experience and vested interest in a job, but it does not insure good judgment and creativity in occupations where the test of competence is capacity to think independently and yet work effectively through people. To give seniority much weight slows up the progress of others who perhaps are more competent; and, if the rule is rigidly applied, its influence almost inevitably is reflected sooner or later in a decadent organization and rising levels of mediocrity.

Valid objections may be interposed against too stubborn adherence to any rule. The customary practice in organizations of always following the formal channels of command in transmitting orders from above or receiving communications from below, endlessly passing needed papers back and forth, illustrates this point. As standard practice, this amenity possesses the great virtue of maintaining order, but it sometimes results in stuffy formality and artificiality. Its habitual observance almost completely precludes personal contact between members of the high command and the bright young men who, in every healthy organization, occupy the lower echelons of management, those storehouses of future executive talent which should never become depleted and whose promising occupants must never be overlooked.

One of the critical problems confronting the central executive authority in almost all large organizations is how to maintain adequate relationships and encouragement from top to bottom throughout the managerial structure. Every conscientious executive feels a constant need to know his people. Their strengths and weaknesses, their aspirations and disappointments, their latent potential, the motivations which kindle them into action are the stuff out of which teamwork must be evolved. Yet organizational conventions, unless resisted and made to serve rather than master, sometimes contrive to set up impenetrable barriers and stratification which can eventually strangle progress.

The appearance of personal success and the elegant surroundings naturally associated with high executive positions in many "fine old companies" often generate more stagnation than innovation. Advancing years, maturing experience, tenure, and security, it is ordinarily assumed (occasionally with a modicum of justification), are natural accompaniments of wisdom; but it is one of the quirks of human nature that they do not always encourage personal resourcefulness in equal measure. Constant reminders of having "arrived" give most men little incentive to strive still harder and improve even upon a distinguished past.

This precious attribute of being forever on the look-out for new problems to solve is apparently more common to younger and fresher minds. And, in the typical organizational environment, these are likely to be considerably removed from the dignified surroundings of the front office.

Professor Albert B. Stewart,[2] commenting on this phenomenon in scientific fields, where creativity seems to be most in evidence in the modern world, has observed that the age at which great physicists make their first discoveries has shown no tendency to increase since the beginning of the century—this in spite of the numbing thought that there is so much more already known to be learned at the start! The men in this field most closely identified with each of the first six decades of this century, he points out, have all been in their twenties when they made the contribution for which they are primarily noted. One wonders how these youthful leaders in scientific thought would have fared in the environment of the modern corporate organization. Would they have been identified and encouraged sufficiently?

As the corporate community of interest which comprises the individual enterprise grows, and as its activities become more complex, it is not long before management must determine quite formally how each member of the group can best make his contribution to the joint effort in a way that will still permit harmonious action on the part of the team as though with one mind. Operations at this precise moment acquire new dimensions. Traditions, conventional practices, systems, and formal

[2] Stewart, Albert B., Professor of Physics, Antioch College, writing on "How Liberal an Education," *Antioch Notes*, Vol. 39, No. 6 (March 1962).

instructions begin to emerge as they do in all corporate entities, in business or elsewhere, contributing their indispensable sense of fitness.

It is important, at this juncture in the evolution of the organization, that there be strenuous resistance to the building of artificial barriers within the structure which will hinder the discovery of hidden values and discourage the worthy. Ways must always be found for putting rare talents for innovation and creative thinking to work wherever they are. Without them, future prospects are barren indeed—for there can be no progress, no promise of permanence, either in the individual firm or, for that matter, in the economic life of society as a whole.

X

The Executive's Adjustment to His Environment

HUMAN BEINGS, OF ALL NATURE'S CREATURES, SEEM TO POSSESS IN marked degree the quite special capacity to make unaided adjustments to a changing environment. But, what is even more significant, men continually adjust this environment to their own purposes. The ability to do so always increases the hazards of making mistakes—from which lesser forms of life apparently are immune—but it also makes possible important breaks in the continuity of past, present, and future events.

Maintaining reasonable objectivity in analyzing the heritage with which each generation is saddled permits acceptance of what seems good but rejection of that which is inconsistent with the environmental model which has been constructed for emulation. This power of choice and redirection of future events is, of course, at the root of all progress.

The role of executives, like that of all participants in the social order, must be interpreted with intelligence. It is essential that they understand the setting in which the action of the play takes place. The social environment in which executives operate always presupposes some distinctive philosophy of economic organization, and the basic assumptions supporting this particular philosophy must be generally accepted.

This environment also is conditioned by what has gone before. It is influenced by the tradition of past business practice; by the degree to which past behavior has fallen short of compliance with this acceptable philosophy; by the correctives that have been and are being applied to past deficiencies; by what yet remains to be done before ultimate achievement of desired goals. These are major influences to which executives must either make adjustment or direct events into channels more to their liking.

The economic philosophy and organizational pattern generally accepted in the Western World are quite distinctive. There is no reconciling them with rival beliefs held elsewhere with equal fervor. Seldom before in human history have contrasting ideologies been so sharply drawn upon so grand a scale. Seldom have they been defended so tenaciously. Seldom have they so dominated the minds of their adherents.

The contrasting specifications of these rival beliefs are readily stated. Defense of private enterprise never need make us ashamed, for in spirit it is equated with the essentials of human dignity. It is based upon the premise, no matter how neglected in practice, that each individual is important; that his personal aspirations are not to be totally submerged in the assumed interests of the state.

True believers in this doctrine can readily agree that individual welfare is never exclusively dependent upon, or identified with, any single human right or privilege. All such natural rights, it seems most probable, eventually stand or fall together. Each is expressed through its own particular institutional media; each has its own characteristic appeal; but all serve universal human and highly personal needs.

The Communist world, in contrast, grants the individual no such importance. His entire existence tends instead to be rudely drawn into the web of a collectivist regime, dominated at the center by an authoritative group presumed, as long as it can continue to stay in power, to be omniscient. The resulting monolithic corporate state has little use for private ownership; it restricts individual choice almost to the vanishing point.

These two opposed economic and political systems, set apart so completely by their respective philosophies, have no such differences in their approaches to the physical world. Private capitalism and communism may be bitter rivals indefinitely in their efforts to inherit the earth, but in exploiting its resources they follow parallel paths.

Industry, wherever found in either system, is necessarily concerned with application of the engineering sciences to concrete business uses. It depends upon natural resources and the way they are utilized. It is concerned with technical processes; with input and output relationships in the manufacturing plant; with operating efficiency, waste prevention, and product yields. Upon these factors the possibility of achieving national productive goals depends. But eventually, if the productive process is ever to rise above the dead level of a meaningless treadmill existence, the wishes of consumers must be served.

Seven Basic Assumptions of Free Enterprise

Yet it is not in these materialistic aspects of industry that the two economic and political systems differ so sharply. The unique philosophy of private enterprise is to be found instead in spiritual aspirations mellowing the economic interrelations of men. The major postulates of this system of enterprise may be summarized as follows:

1. *There must be a universally accepted standard of personal morality and mutual trust insuring the sanctity of contracts.* Men must rely on each other and behave honestly beyond the reach of legal compulsion. Where personal guarantees cannot be trusted, there is no solid basis for negotiation nor hope of stable relationships.

2. *The structure of society, it is assumed, is pluralistic.* The various aspirations which civilized men cherish and the means by which they seek to acquire power sufficient for their fulfillment are presumed to occupy separate compartments in the social organization. Nothing, for example, is more deeply imbedded in our national heritage or zealously accorded more nearly universal approval than the separation of church and state. The separation of politics as the normal sphere of government from economics as vested in business enterprise also is a basic assumption of classic liberal doctrine, though obviously it is never perfectly realized.

Economic developments always have political consequences, and political decisions are a constant restraint upon economic

forces. Holders of economic power continually seek to influence
the political climate just as holders of political power seek to
make the economic environment conform to their own concepts
of the general welfare.

No one need be reminded of this present tendency. We are
continually told that intervention of an omnipresent federal
government in the supposed promotion of nearly all phases of
individual existence is essential even though, because of distance, familiarity with the local scene must necessarily be quite
general and impersonal. It is as though these centralized powers
were somehow imbued with a higher form of wisdom and compassion. This remote intervention, it is contended, inevitably
must supplant or at the very best subordinate local efforts to
deal with what in most respects are distinctly local problems.

The central government unquestionably becomes more and
more powerful and ubiquitous. Its intrusion upon what in times
past were private matters is ever more insistent. Its tax demands, by standards thought tolerable less than a lifetime ago,
are beyond belief. Private institutions and local governments
subject to the pre-emptive claims of the central treasury increasingly cast covetous eyes upon federal subsidies. To all of them,
this central treasury seems to have become inexhaustible, re-
plenished though it is from what were initially their own local
resources.

That these sentiments are the natural outgrowth of the inordi-
nate social stresses of modern times is somewhat beside the
point. The problems are real and their solution is baffling, but
there are serious dangers in encouraging private and local public institutions to lean upon an all-embracing and supposedly
benevolent central state. Political opportunists, skilled in fan-
ning the natural cupidity of pressure groups whose voting
strength is formidable, seize upon such issues in the name of
individual rights and social justice.

The tragedy is that this means of remedy gradually saps individual and local community desire to accept the pains of self-
help. It fans the ever-insistent personal craving for security,
frequently in those who may not be very deserving. And eventually it is used to rationalize disbelief in the adequacies of private
and local efforts to deal with pressing social problems. It is less

than candid to brand as incorrigible reactionaries all who feel some twinge of misgiving concerning this curiously inverted doctrine of many modern liberals.

Peter F. Drucker,[1] speaking upon some aspects of this general theme, has pointed out quite explicitly the grave dangers which throughout history have beset every pluralist society like our own. When private power blocks come into headlong conflict with public interests, there is no question which must in the end prevail. It has never much mattered where these threats come from. It may have been, in times long past, some special group of medicine men possessed of magic powers. It sometimes has been—and could be again—a too strongly entrenched priesthood, a military élite, a group with aristocratic pretensions striving to perpetuate itself. It could be a self-disciplined labor bloc under too ambitious leadership, a political party flushed with apparent success in drawing together powerful special interests at election time and so rendering ineffective the constructive benefits of our two-party system. To some, the threat seems chiefly to come from corporate business wielding oppressive economic power.

Whatever the source, the baleful influence is the same. Ultimately, says Drucker, survival has invariably been threatened when the public interest could only be imposed on these power centers by supporting them—or else their self-interest choked the public interest and destroyed society.

3. *Our enterprise system expressly assumes an elaborate framework of political surveillance over private affairs.* There must be an equitable system of laws impartially enforced to protect property, maintain order, and insure nonviolent settlement of disputes. Without this restraining influence, the business firm is helpless. Innovators soon become discouraged. Investors hastily withdraw.

4. *There must be an implicit belief in the prophylactic influence of competition as an instrument of economic control.* True competition does not, as moralists sometimes seem to think, necessarily imply complete acceptance of the harsh doctrine of the survival of the fittest. Neither does it permit price main-

[1] Drucker, Peter F., "Big Business and Public Policy," Filene lecture at Roosevelt University, 1962. Published in *Business and Society,* Vol. 3, No. 1 (1962).

tenance by deliberate agreement among the strong—for their own advantage, to be sure, but resulting nevertheless in a protective covering for the weak and inefficient. Either course leads in the end to destroying competition as a corrective force. The true intent is always to maintain it.

The essential ingredient in all competition, whether of price, product design, quality, or service, lies in the determination of every contender to meet or better, if he can, the terms on which his rivals offer to do business. Free competition, as a controlling market force, is the exact opposite of dependence upon cartels to fix prices and share the market by prearrangement.

It is too much to expect that among competitors there will ever be precise equality of ability, of power, of fortune, or of circumstance. But to maintain among men an approximate equality of opportunity to achieve whatever their respective talents allow is a practical goal. Given so powerful an incentive, human ingenuity, if permitted sufficient latitude, can doubtless be relied upon to maintain the purging fires of competition. This expectation, when applied to corporate affairs, is the justification of all sound antitrust legislation and its administration—a distinctly American experiment in economic regulation.

That the competitive race need not always be won only by the huge or strong, provided equality of opportunity is preserved, is perhaps one of the most encouraging signs in modern American industry. As leading economist Arthur F. Burns [2] has observed, the outstanding social achievement of our times has been the expansion of economic opportunity. Small and independent businesses continue to be an important gateway to this opportunity despite the giant corporations that seem at times to surround us. Over four and a half million independent concerns are presently engaged in various types of business, and their number is growing. There are more business firms today, both absolutely and in relation to the size of the nation's workforce, than there were ten, twenty, or thirty years ago.

5. *Private enterprise recognizes the essentiality of risk taking as a stimulus to technological progress.* It has long been assumed that the burden of taking risks bears most heavily upon

[2] Drawn from "The Expansion of Economic Opportunity," a convocation address at the University of Chicago in September 1960.

ownership, from which it follows as a sort of Golden Rule of property ownership that where the risk lies there should also be control of the particular form this risk should take.

This traditional right of owners to manage their affairs and, as a counterpart of this right, the obligation to take risks, are implicit in simple business relationships, though subject to considerable qualification in modern corporate practice. The expectation that those with venture capital to invest will gain in the event of success just as they will inevitably suffer loss in event of failure is no longer always wholly valid. The popular disposition to condemn legitimate profit taking as "profiteering," plus the equalization of personal rewards that has been so effectively achieved by steeply graduated income taxes, has unquestionably made its influence felt. These new factors in our economy tend to discourage risk taking as a universally recognized ingredient in a vigorous system of enterprise. And this at the very time when our rate of economic growth, it is often contended, is so far short of desired goals.

Risk taking in business is, of course, not exclusively the burden of investors. In modern industry, the vested interest of employees in their jobs is actually not much subordinate, if at all, in any acceptable scale of values to the vested interest of owners in their shareholdings. Certainly the prospect of losing one's job in an economic setting where occupational mobility is lacking may become a personal misfortune of the first water. It is no less tragic than the experience of the investor when faced with the prospect of losing his savings. Because both are risk takers in a very real sense, it is possible to argue with some appearance of logic—spurious though it is—that both owners and employees ought to have the privilege of direct participation in management decisions and the power of veto when these decisions affect their respective destinies.

There is no denying the fact that the rewards of risk taking, whether in dividends or wages, should be related to the magnitude of the risk to which the recipient is exposed. Nor should employers be surprised if, when the well-known hazards of technological unemployment appear, employees insist upon some form of compensation consistent with the acute nature of this risk which modern labor is called upon to assume. The important thing is that compliance with these demands must not be permitted to destroy risk taking itself.

6. *There must be a concerted effort by everyone to preserve the right and privilege of voluntary participation in the economic order in the hope of sharing in its rewards.* A free economy must, in short, be free. All who are associated with a business firm, whether as stockholders, employees, creditors, suppliers, or customers, must of their own volition be privileged to withdraw their support when they are no longer in sympathy with it. This personal right of decision not to associate in any private endeavor, no matter what it may be, is fundamental.

Freedom of association is without a doubt one of the most precious and pervasive freedoms for every individual, touching his life at all points in business and social relationships of every sort. It is at the same time one of the most difficult to maintain. Freedom to sever associations no longer desired is never much questioned, but freedom to enter new associations as a matter of personal privilege is something quite different. Harmonious associations in business, whether they involve relationships between employers and employees, creditors and debtors, or buyers and sellers, necessarily depend upon bilateral agreement. The most that can be hoped for is that decisions on either side shall be based upon considerations of personal merit and be devoid of prejudice. And this goal, obviously, relies for achievement more upon the civilized goodwill of individuals than upon legislation.

7. *Benefits must be shared fairly in proportion to the respective contributions of all participants in the individual firm's operations.* Effective incentives demand this. Common justice in all cooperative efforts requires that rewards be related to personal *deserts,* not personal *wants,* which so often have a subtle way of becoming personal *needs,* which in turn readily give way to insistence that benefits which started out to be merely personal desires are really indisputable personal *rights.*

Numerous individuals and quite diverse power groups, as previously observed, claim attention as participants in every firm's operations. Each contributes significantly to its welfare. Investors provide means of support for the firm's program. Employees provide needed manpower. Suppliers provide raw materials and services. Customers generate sales demand. The forces of government, through its police powers, stand ready to maintain order.

Each of these contributing groups competes for a "fair" share in the rewards of enterprise in the individual firm—a fair return on investment, fair pay, a fair deal in purchase commitments (thus giving rise to questions of reciprocity in intercompany negotiations), fair prices, fair tax levies for the privilege of doing business. The pressures come from every side, forever insistent, and maintaining them all in balance is a constant concern of management. And since, in a private enterprise system, the state of the economy as a whole always depends upon the stability of its numerous parts, the equitable distribution of the firm's gross revenues among these various claimants is vital both to the individual firm and to the economy as a whole. No other responsibility of management is so demanding of complete objectivity and the ability to achieve acceptable compromises.

The Mixed Legacy of Modern Business

These several tenets of free enterprise—often, or so it seems, in peril from centralist tendencies—are the bedrock of the private business executive's creed. They are in no small measure within executive keeping in each generation. As the basic conditions on which private enterprise can be conducted, they enjoy widespread if not universal acceptance among us as matters of abstract principle. And yet private business seems to be forever on trial.

The sharpest arrows clearly are leveled by the critics of private enterprise not at its moral objectives, and certainly not at its material achievements, but at what are alleged to be defects of organization which fail to correct the natural shortcomings of human behavior. Corporate reputations which, under modern conditions, determine the degree of popular approval or disapproval enjoyed by private enterprise, often suffer from the excesses indulged in by their predecessors. Institutions no more than individuals can wholly escape accusations of guilt by association. The stain of past misdemeanors, even when not the responsibility of anyone now living, continues to require expiation. As products of an evolutionary process, the reputations of either individuals or corporate groups are linked firmly to what their forerunners have been. Business executives in particular need continually to remind themselves of past shortcomings in business morality lest these be repeated.

Huge economic units clothed with corporate license and manipulated by designing and willful men began to attract especial notice in American business in the latter half of the nineteenth century. The times were ripe for this development. The nation sought to rally from the appalling struggle of civil war. Resources in abundance awaited exploitation. As in the aftermath of every great war, young men were restless and impatient of order and restraint, and the resulting excesses in many respects were bound to leave a dubious legacy.

The wealth of forests, mines, and newly developed oil fields; new techniques in transportation; the accelerated demand for products which farmers sold and for products which farmers were beginning to buy—signs in almost every field, in fact, pointed unmistakably to a rebirth of industry. These developments, moreover, were unhampered by the technological limitations of earlier and simpler days. Corporate boundaries soon were no longer confined to localized communities or subject to the jurisdictions of local governments, and the Federal Government was as yet ill equipped to assume control.

This new-found private power, this relative release from governmental restraint, this tempting opportunity to exploit resources and, for the first time, with the technological means of doing so could hardly help but result in grave abuses. By today's more civilized standards of business conduct, they indeed seem shameful. Enormous personal fortunes, untouched by oppressive taxation, quickly accumulated. Low wages, long hours, and sordid working conditions were not yet thought incongruous with this concentrated wealth.

Here was a social environment in which inequities in living standards were sometimes regarded as manifestations of God's inscrutable will. Contempt for public interests comes naturally when governmental restraints are lax. Even the spokesmen of organized religion often were strangely silent on these earthly matters. The puritan virtues of thrift, sobriety, and diligence in business—which this new managerial élite certainly possessed in superlative degree—were held by many in this early Victorian age to be next to godliness. Recurrent rumblings of labor unrest, in contrast, were likely to be frowned upon as almost sacrilegious by these same pillars of the existing order. What right had "stupid" workmen to assume that they could rise *en masse* above their predestined station? Such sentiments, however strange to modern thought, were readily associated with hardy individualism by men still not far removed from the mores of a frontier society.

But the pendulum which had swung so far past center presently was bound to reverse direction. "Individual worth" was not simply an empty phrase. Was not the Declaration of Independence—the very birth certificate of the Republic, less than three generations old—based on the belief that "men are created equal"?

The new century was, in fact, scarcely begun when Theodore Roosevelt, who was always dramatic but had an unerring instinct for human decency, launched his "trust busting" program. This continued in a quieter key, but possibly more effectively, as it gained momentum in the antitrust efforts of his successors. The best intellects of the day, stirred by a new sense of social responsibility, declaimed against unhealthy concentrations of economic power in private hands. And presently, in the Supreme Court, the social wisdom of Holmes and Brandeis, first uttered in dissent, eventually became the prevailing view. Thus, in these stirring times, the executive, legislative, and judicial departments of the government evolved a new philosophy respecting the relationship of government to corporate business which eventually was fixed indelibly within the American system.

And there were other social ferments, beginning to build up pressure, which paralleled these new concepts in law and morals. Labor, chafing from ancient wrongs, managed to develop able champions after abortive and bloody struggles to improve the wage earner's status. Men like Samuel Gompers were spokesmen and organizers who could appeal to reason, arouse emotions, mobilize their followers in strength, and make their power felt. Out of great travail they laid the foundations upon which subsequent leaders have gradually fashioned a new and formidable contender in the business community. Big labor in today's world feels no apologetic sense of inferiority in contending with big business.

In technology also, a small group of creative production engineers, including such men as Frederick W. Taylor, H. L. Gantt, and Frank B. Gilbreth, were demonstrating that low labor costs were not dependent upon low wages. This strange new idea—which is at the very root of all technological progress—was presently to be put to test in an industry just being born.

A new school of industrialists with Henry Ford in its vanguard understood that mass production could get nowhere without its counterpart, mass consumption. The purchasing power of the common man had somehow to be improved in depth. It was equally plain to these prophets of a new industrial order how the task must be accomplished. Individual productivity had to be increased. Better methods of performance had to be devised. Mechanical energies had to be harnessed in novel ways and applied in the form of better, more powerful tools. The long and disturbing trend toward industrial automation was thus given new impetus.

In almost every field of endeavor, the changing picture served to cast management in new roles, to suggest new concepts of economic thought, to place new emphasis upon innovation, to create new attitudes toward the marketing process. The ultimate result was wider distribution of the abundance which these new and yeasty ideas were helping to create.

The reverse swing of the pendulum, as with all momentous social changes by which men seek to build a more satisfying way of life, obviously did not come suddenly. The excesses of a lusty past revealed by even these casual reminders of unattractive relics in corporate closets naturally left deep scars that still have not been erased. These doubtless help to explain the gross misconceptions, innuendoes, valid suspicions, and latent fears concerning corporate morals that are still in evidence among the public.

The Worst Possible Interpretation

The present day may be truthfully characterized as a full-blown industrial age. Everyone depends upon its bounties. Yet it is always easy to find those who are eager to accept the worst possible interpretation of businessmen's motives and of corporate behavior.

The late Claude Robinson,[3] who had more than ordinary opportunities to sound the trends in public thought, observed only a few weeks before his death that the concept of profit is widely misunderstood. People, he found, can agree in the abstract upon the "necessity and desirability" of profits as one of the "key institutions of a capitalistic order." But even—and sometimes, it seems, almost especially—in supposedly enlightened circles, "profit is frequently cast in the role of the villain" as being "synonymous with 'exploitation.'" Profits, Robinson wrote, are frequently alluded to as "too big, monopolistic, unfair, or antisocial," without benefit of knowledgeable standards by which these characterizations can be substantiated. And few if any outside business circles, he lamented, take the trouble to come to their defense.

Men in high places continually deplore the inflationary effect of corporate price increases, but who in positions of political influence show the same concern about wage increases? Yet these also, if not compensated for by increased productivity or price inflation, contribute to the "profit squeeze."

Similar misgivings are clearly manifest in public disapproval of corporate bigness. Competition, it is alleged, ceases to be a controlling force when industrial giants insolently divide the market into their respective spheres of influence and contrive to stabilize prices through carefully concealed "gentlemen's agreements."

In the 1930's, when the nation struggled to recover from deep depression, economists of great repute, supported by exhausting and disturbing statistical proof, thought they saw—and in the

[3] Robinson, Claude, *Understanding Profits*, D. Van Nostrand Company, 1961.

not too distant future—the inevitable concentration of an over-whelming proportion of the nation's productive effort within the control of a very few powerful and potentially relentness corpo-rations. And the trends, reduced to numerical terms, lent credi-bility to these predictions. The public mind, still smarting from disillusionment, accepted them without much critical question. Impersonal corporations seemed a convenient scapegoat on which to unload bitter personal disappointments. Had not the abysmal decline in the value of corporate securities wiped out the paper profits which only a short time before seemed to almost everyone proof positive of his own financial wizardry?

It was a time when political capital could be made out of not too vague references to "princes of privilege" and "malefac-tors of great wealth." This was campaign oratory, to be sure, not to be taken very seriously by the enlightened but still a goad to "financiers" so recently rudely awakened.

Hindsight, as always, reveals some new factors in the econ-omy which few, if any, could have had the foresight to see. The enormously improved bargaining status of wage earners, the leveling influence of steeply graduated income taxes made neces-sary by the nation's renewed war efforts, the widespread institu-tionalized investments in corporate equities already were begin-ning to influence wealth distribution and make envy-stirring epithets archaic.

That the dolorous predictions have not materialized, at least in the time allotted for realization by the prophets, is fairly clear. Corporations have continued to grow in size, but the econ-omy as measured in deflated dollars has also experienced a mushroom growth. Small businesses multiply and sometimes prosper. In industries harboring giant corporations, there are only a few in which the leaders today occupy the same relative position of dominance they enjoyed three or four decades ago.

If competition is dead, in short, most corporate executives apparently have not discovered it. If, in an age when market news is communicated instantaneously, price uniformity seems to suggest less price competition, there is still unabated compe-tition in alternative products, in service, and in the constant im-provement of both through research.

The Modern Executive's Challenge

Potent factors, possibly more clearly discernible with the passing years, seem to have made these alarmist predictions less likely to be fulfilled.

There is, first of all, the influence of what Mr. Justice Holmes once called the brooding omnipresence of the antitrust laws. Few men, save those incurring the heavy penalties that follow upon violation and discovery, would greatly change this heritage. It is part of our national way of life, something quite special in the annals of commerce, differing sharply from the cartel-ridden philosophies and business thought of prewar Western Europe. It is believed in and supported by men of all political persuasions. When managements, through stupidity or misadventure, become entangled in the resulting prohibitions, they receive little sympathy in press or public forum.

Antitrust regulations, therefore, are a fixture in modern business life, but they do create serious problems for the company executive. An ambitious Department of Justice anxious to build a reputation for trust breaking, rivalry among the several needlessly diffuse regulatory agencies for leadership in law enforcement, or even headline-seeking harassment by Congressmen with antibusiness predilections for their own political reasons can be decidedly unsettling in the business community. And the results, administratively speaking—no matter how well intentioned— are not always completely consistent with the professed objectives of the antitrust laws.

People need to be reminded that the hard facts of economics rather than devious tendencies may explain the behavioral patterns which competitors on occasion develop. Instead of the brazen defiance of the law which their actions are said to represent, these may be honest attempts to maintain position within a maze of legal restrictions that is not entirely appropriate for the kind of business that is growing up.

When, under these circumstances, business is indicted, it is the obligation of corporate executives to see that this opposite point of view, when valid, is presented with unfailing energy to the court. Valid claims of justice clearly do not rest upon sure pun-

ishment of technical violations of laws which do not exactly fit
the case at hand. Rather, they rest upon the need for bringing to
account violations based upon deliberate and unsocial intent to
circumvent a law which informed men of goodwill can agree
does fit the case.

The continuing effectiveness of the antitrust laws clearly depends upon the same factors that are essential for keeping all
laws clear and accurate reflections of life as it really is. Balanced judicial decisions resulting in "good law" seldom are
arrived at by undefended actions or "consent decrees" grudg-
ingly agreed to by defendants as the cheapest way out of the
difficulty in which they find themselves. Sometimes, instead,
these common occurrences result in legal precedents without
either judge or public learning what is really basic in the case.

A second, equally powerful restraint on corporate behavior
arises from the fact that concentrations of managerial power
develop their own antidote. Big business is today only one contender in the economic struggle. When it is tempted to excesses,
there is always in the offing the counterbalancing force of big
labor, equally powerful, equally arrogant, and equally contemptuous of public convenience though not yet invariably subject to
the sobering influence of government disapproval.

One of these titans inevitably breeds the other. One checkmates
and disciplines the other. When they are locked in conflict, each
strives for the aid and comfort to be derived from whatever
measure of public approval each can muster.

Moreover, the power of big business is further counterbalanced by big government. This opposing force is not necessarily
applied directly through the use of police powers. Often it may
be as effectively brought to bear indirectly, through governmental purchasing power. For big government is industry's greatest
customer by far.

It is not essential to the public interest that governmental
purchases be widely distributed in the first instance. What does
it matter in actual fact if the enormous acquisitions made by a
procurement sector like the Department of Defense are deliberately negotiated with a mere handful of corporate giants? How
else could the job be done so expeditiously in any sort of enterprise system? Who is deprived of participation in the resulting

business under our particular economic system when prime contracts are, in turn, fanned out in a vast network of subcontracts? In one form or another these secondary purchasing arrangements actually generate local company payrolls in nearly every community in the land.

The true signifiance of this physical decentralization of industrial activity with centralized prime contract negotiations can as yet hardly be fathomed. It has been made possible by wholesale application of a time-tested engineering principle: the interchangeability of product components. Subcontracting arrangements, subject to rigid engineering specifications, have thus become a profoundly significant development in our economy.

The highly integrated pattern of production which has resulted first received great impetus in the total mobilization of American industry in two World Wars. It is one of the really basic changes in industrial organization and technology in modern times. Because of it, small corporations of limited means can still multiply and prosper in the very shadow of the corporate giants which so often are the major focus of public fears and attention.

And the new pattern is not by any means confined exclusively to government business. When the three or four corporate leaders in the motor industry, for example, are dependent upon small industries as suppliers throughout the Middle West and even in areas farther removed—just as these same small operations depend upon their big contemporaries as major customers —the concept of corporate interdependence in modern private enterprise takes on new dimensions. For this network of contractual relationships is something quite different from the monolithic concentration of private economic power in a few vertically integrated monster corporations which our economic system once threatened to become and is still often popularly pictured to be.

Possibly, too, there is still a third major deterrent to the excesses resulting from concentrated corporate power. This lies in the changing attitudes and mores of executives themselves. The motivation which dominated the powerful barons of corporate business three-quarters of a century ago apparently was quite direct and simple. They sought above all else the gratification of personal power and the accumulation of personal wealth. Seldom did they give much indication of acute personal distress over glaring maldistributions of material goods. Their own economic progress was not disturbed by the leveling influence of onerous taxation levied upon either income or inheritance.

Purchases of labor were not thought of in significantly different terms from commodity procurement. Dealings in the marketplace, whether in buying services or materials, seem to have been strictly an exercise behooving wage earners and suppliers always to be on guard. Similarly, minority stockholders and owners whose operations these industrial overlords covetously sought to bring into their own corporate orbit were likely to find themselves mere pawns in a business proceeding which they could neither control nor understand. This was owner-management in its most virulent form.

A few corporate entities, though they are a distinctly vanishing type in big business, still qualify as family enterprises in which the founders' descendents continue to be the dominant element in management as well as ownership. But it is more usual, particularly in seasoned enterprises offering corporate equities worth the attention of outside investors, for major ownership concentrations to be identified with institutional stockholders—investment trusts, pension and endowment funds, foundations, and other professionally managed investment portfolios. Such institutional investors characteristically seek only an assured return and develop little taste for corporate power. They rarely interfere with management; and, in the event their investment proves less than satisfactory, they would sooner retire from the field than undertake managerial improvements.

These well-known trends in corporate ownership are, in effect, contributing to a gradual emancipation of corporate management. They will, in time, quite likely cause significant changes in executive outlook. But this new-found standard of corporate morality, important as it is bound to be, will never obviate the necessity of looking critically at the deficiencies and mistaken judgments of *people*—of executives as well as others. The satisfactions of our social and economic order depend upon unprejudiced disciplining of private interests.

Vigilance is always the price of uninterrupted institutional existence. No living enterprise seems ever to be free of persistent calls, on one pretext or another, for reform.

The important thing in seeking needed correctives is to make sure that the prescription is calculated to neutralize the underlying foolishness of individuals. It would be tragic if, instead, the cumulative effects of ill-assorted nostrums were ultimately to destroy the system. Institutional shortcomings, because they reflect human imperfections, are subject to remedy. For individuals, no matter how important they appear to themselves, rarely enjoy an influence of much more than momentary effect. Some in every organization aspire for a time to be assigned the role of leading man in the select company of their local firm, but in the vast setting of free enterprise, no single executive ever plays more than momentarily anything except a minor supporting role.

XI

The Development of Executive Potential

IT IS NEVER EASY TO DETERMINE AT ARM'S LENGTH, SO TO SPEAK, WHY one organization becomes an exciting success while another which apparently has equal initial opportunities fails to arouse enthusiasm. It seems to make little difference what the particular enterprise may be—whether gardening, let us say, or baseball, or business.

One gardener, for instance, succeeds in creating a thing of marvelous beauty. Another, blessed with the same fertile soil, seems forever thwarted by an endless battle with weeds and vermin. Two ball clubs start out each spring with clean slates. One ends the season far down in the second division. The other is consistently a contender for first place. Two businesses are founded in the same decade, in the same industry, on what appears to be an equal footing. A generation later, one is twice as large and five times as profitable as the other.

Chance, obviously, plays some part in these contrasting pictures. A particularly favorable combination of sun and rainfall, well timed, may occasionally save a gardener's efforts from impending disaster. But the rain falls and the sun shines on all gardeners alike. "Lucky breaks" sometimes determine the outcome of a ball game. But the winner must seize the initiative and turn his luck to good advantage. Besides, sheer luck never seems a good enough explanation at the end of the season why one club out of ten becomes the pennant winner.

Some stroke of luck may in time of crisis enable a struggling business to pay its bills and get off to a new start on a successful career. But it takes more than chance to account for the fact that one business, years later, never needs to reach beyond its own borders for executive replacements, while in another which started out with equal opportunities executives seem always on parade, coming and going in search of more satisfying connections.

That wise old English gardener probably was not far from the mark, though obviously guilty of oversimplification, when he attributed his success to "good seed and loving care." Certainly this modest prescription has in it more substance than the popular "green thumb" theory of success.

When one digs beneath the surface in any successful business, some executive is almost sure to be found who is personally interested in maintaining a systematic recruiting program and in seeing that those selected to participate in it have ample opportunities to grow. Many years ago, for example, the chief executive of a vast merchandising enterprise proposed that his company embark on a new executive training program to forestall what he believed to be an impending crisis in its growth. He stated the problem and provided the solution with simple clarity.

"It is essential," he admonished his executive associates, "that we plan for still greater accomplishments. Our main reliance," said he, "must always be on men. These comprise our greatest riches. Nothing else happens in this business that compares in importance with what happens in each store every day, with monotonous regularity, under the watchful eye of a good store manager.

"We at this policy level of our organization have no greater responsibility than—

- Selecting those marked for advancement with the utmost care.
- Disciplining them with firmness.
- Rewarding them with liberality.
- Backing them up with competent replacements.
- Providing them with opportunities to broaden their experience.

- Encouraging them to develop their full potential as executives.

"We must do these things without fail," he concluded, "so that our good fortune may continue."

Executive Manpower the Prime Problem of Modern Business

The first requirement, as this chief executive indicated, is the selection of men capable of development. A systematic recruitment program is essential, and all possible sources of good candidates must be carefully explored.

It is a common saying among educators that colleges select students, but students also select colleges. The observation applies as well to industrial recruitment. No one knows for certain at the beginning of any young man's career how high he will prove capable of rising in the managerial structure. But the techniques for predicting executive potential are sufficiently reliable to permit employers to seek out and attract those giving most promise of success.

The real test, of course, comes subsequently in the organization's ability to hold men worthy of being held. Recruitment of itself is futile if, after the exhilaration of new employment dies down, the best men leave and ten years later only those least likely to succeed remain. Men of superior qualifications in the executive market always have a wide freedom of choice as to where they will work. They will not be content to stay for long unless the surroundings are congenial, initiative is encouraged, personal associations are stimulating, and achievement is rewarded.

The intent of every well-maintained organization is to find suitable replacements for top executive positions within the firm. New blood is always essential, but it should be introduced at lower levels in the organization. The selected recruits, not as finished executives ready to assume heavy responsibilities but as young men of potential, can be watched carefully for evidences of growth and can be encouraged by opportunities to test their capabilities for leadership. This process of executive development, to be successful, requires sustained and systematic effort. It is never a matter of haphazardly gathering together bits and pieces of pertinent information or of filling empty vessels standing passively in line. It demands concentrated effort by each individual throughout his lifetime.

Professor Herbert A. Simon [1] has reminded us that human beings come into the world endowed unequally in physical appearance, in mental alertness and sensory perception, and in disposition. To a considerable extent, most aspects of this initial endowment can be measured and improved. The inborn talents which permit a man to excel as an athlete, a scientist, an artist, a musician, or an executive are personal possessions. They are scarcely discernible at the outset, but they may by dint of learning, practice, and experience eventually be developed into mature skills.

Executive skills, even though clearly dependent upon prolonged experience, can be perfected more rapidly in candidates who have had exposure to a well-conceived program of formal education. Every successful business enterprise, intent as it must be upon recruiting and developing its executive potential, must today be sympathetically allied with the vast national resources of advanced education. Complete reliance upon apprenticeship manifestly is no longer any more tenable for business executives than for lawyers, doctors, or engineers. Respectable collegiate credentials are rapidly becoming prerequisites for recognition and advancement.

But for the finished "professional," no matter what his academic certification or natural bent may be, there is no substitute for the supplementary requirement of arduous practice and experience. The organization, no matter how fortunate in recruitment, which succeeds in "growing its own" executives must always give dedicated attention to its in-plant executive training activities, reinforcing and continuing the educational achievements of its recruits prior to their joining the organization.

Executive training admittedly has become fashionable in modern business and is undertaken in many ways. Sometimes programs include carefully prepared text materials presenting

[1] Simon, Herbert A., *The New Science of Management Decision,* Harper & Brothers, 1960.

technical information which someone in authority believes every supervisor or executive should know. Sometimes a fairly extensive course of formal class instruction is set up, and sometimes a large and costly corps of training specialists is organized to do the job. It is of the utmost importance to realize that no one of these methods, or even all three together, will insure effective executive development.

A common mistake of educational endeavors is too much emphasis upon what is fancied to be teaching and not enough upon learning. The goal of developing executive potential is unlikely to be achieved by relegating the task to a staff group of training specialists, no matter how eager and dedicated and intelligent they may be. They may know all about how to teach, but may themselves have little to teach.

The techniques of recruitment, testing, and selection may provide better than average chances of success in finding likely candidates. Attentive handling after employment will unquestionably shorten the path of these beginners to the desired goal. Means for measuring progress possibly can be discovered so that young men of promise are not often lost or forgotten in the organization. But, if the novice eventually succeeds in developing his full potential as a competent and finished executive, it will have been largely through his own application. Others can only give him opportunities for self-help.

Executive Development Everyone's Responsibility

Actually, responsibility for assisting subordinates by precept but, even more, by example rests heavily upon everyone in authority, whether of the staff or of the line.

The most important contribution a director of training can make to executive development is to promote a deep-seated understanding throughout management of the need for creating an environment in which executive talents are encouraged. He can assist managers in developing an awareness of their own essential role in drawing out the latent abilities of subordinates. He can stimulate the intellectual curiosity of trainees and urge them to take advantage of their opportunities for self-improvement. Beyond this, really fruitful in-plant training—if it is to be reasonably well achieved—is most likely to be found scattered throughout the organization in inspiring working relationships between supervisors and their men.

The intelligent supervisor is always anxious to bring out the best in his subordinates since he progresses as they progress. The intelligent subordinate, in turn, is always anxious to profit from the experience of his superiors. He wastes little time in fretting about whether he is receiving the kind of training he wants, knowing instinctively that intensive cultivation of his ability to do work that he likes is the best insurance of advancement.

It is the dual aim of all valid educational programs, in plant or out, formal or informal, to prepare the beneficiary for his chosen career and to afford opportunity for enjoyment of a fuller and richer existence. The controversy carried on eternally among academicians as to the respective merits of general, vocational, and professional education ought to be easily resolved.

General education is the foundation of all systematic efforts to cultivate men's minds. Its purpose is training for a more complete life. *Vocationalism* aims instead primarily at training students for their first or next job. There is great need for such training. The real issue here is how society may best fulfill this need without too much encroachment, at the expense of higher needs, upon limited educational resources. *Professional education,* in contrast, aims at providing the opportunity to cultivate skills essential for successful practice in the student's chosen lifetime career. It is always geared to some specific occupational environment. It assumes a need for special, intensive preparation to become qualified for success.

For business executives, this discipline presupposes identification with some typical business firm. It is concerned with developing the special skills which executives must acquire if they are to be given responsibility for their firm's success. These responsibilities include setting institutional goals, formulating plans of operation, mobilizing resources, initiating action by assuming command, and setting up an appropriate system for observing, evaluating, and controlling progress toward desired ends.

The executive's environment is actually subject to no very

precise restrictions. It is conditioned by a rigorous climate of *ideas* appropriate to our distinctive system of enterprise. It embraces, always, the appropriation and manipulation of *things* brought into service in response to society's material wants. The business firm in each isolated instance, like all institutions, is also a tightly integrated and purposeful universe of *persons* operating in orbit, as it were, within the boundaries of society at large.

All three of these—an ideology to which executive action needs always to be accommodated, material things which are always or nearly always in limited supply, and human relationships dependent upon a spirit of mutual respect and confidence —give enormous breadth and complexity to the role of executives.

Thus the demands placed upon the executive craft are unusually severe. To be successful, executives must possess emotional balance and steadfast convictions, the intellectual curiosity and probing persistence of men of science, the self-possession of men accustomed to command. The natural conflicts of interest among all who voluntarily join the organization must be brought under control. If the politician's peculiar skill lies in mastery of the mechanics of compromise, then the successful executive and the politician have much in common. Executive training within these comprehensive dimensions is, obviously, something quite beyond "narrow vocationalism."

But how can these special requirements of executive competence be fulfilled? What sort of educational program will best fit aspirants, after further training and experience, to bear these responsibilities? How can executives be imbued with a burning sense of mission?

Comprehensive surveys, quite critical of present-day business education, have pointed out that business executives occupy a field that is still searching for identity and direction.[2] Manage-

[2] Two such studies have recently been published: (*a*) Gordon, Robert Aaron, and Howell, James Edwin, *Higher Education for Business* (the so-called "Ford Report"), Columbia University Press, 1959; and (*b*), Pierson, Frank C., *The Education of American Businessmen* (sponsored by Carnegie Corporation), McGraw-Hill Book Company, Inc., 1959. Both these reports have been competently reviewed by Leonard S. Silk in *The Education of Businessmen*, Supplementary Paper No. 11, Committee for Economic Development, 1960.

ment, it is further observed, is slowly changing from a homely "art" in which tradition and personal hunch have always played an important part. It is beginning instead to justify recognition as a highly skilled and intellectually conditioned calling. It rests upon application of a systematic body of knowledge and techniques relative to business problems.

Management is not a profession if the essential characteristic of a true professional is that exemplified, for instance, in the most respected professions: law and medicine. Practitioners in these fields characteristically offer their services to clients as independent advisers. This unique condition of employment undoubtedly is directly related to many of the concomitants of a degree in law or medicine: official certification of competence, affiliation with a governing vocational association, a code of professional ethics.

The typical business executive is, of course, a full-time employee of some business firm. His employer needs no professional credentials—which, after all, are only technical and superficial badges of achievement—to know how good a man he is. But if, as the late Professor Selekman[3] once said, a major characteristic of those in a profession is a capacity to control emotions so as to achieve a logical analysis of all factors in a complicated problem, then business executives may eventually qualify for this distinction.

The Potential Executive's Progress

The chronological record of the business executive's in-plant career usually approximates the following progression:

1. *Selection and induction*—based, of course, upon someone's judgment of the candidate's potential for growth. The factors most likely to be influential at this time of launching the future executive's career are quite tentative. Impressions, however, are readily formed of the candidate's personal endowments—including such outwardly manifested characteristics as physical stamina, presence,

[3] Selekman, Benjamin M., as quoted in *Harvard Business Review,* July–August 1962, p. 20.

manners, intelligence, emotional stability, educational background, personal interests, and inclination and ambitions respecting desired employment.

2. *Acquisition of technical skills.* Proficiencies of some useful sort must be the candidate's first order of attention. Employment is not offered for the express purpose of educating the employee. Tenure, obviously, is dependent upon proving one's capacity, within a reasonable period, to earn one's pay; and this achievement is first demonstrated by acquiring the necessary technical skills. The first requirement of the apprentice in any craft is to become a journeyman.

3. *Demonstration of supervisory capacity.* The natural path of progression is from recognition as a valued individual performer to acceptance as one able to stimulate good performance in others. This always represents an important landmark in the career of the novice.

4. *Growth in decision-making skill.* The first positive test of executive potential is the development of skill and self-confidence in making decisions and in inspiring cooperation, thereby making one's decisions effective.

5. *Recognized capacity for becoming a "generalist."* This is a mark of distinction quickly recognizable in an environment largely populated by specialists. To be thus identified is unquestionably the crowning achievement in an executive's progress.

It is a common lament of chief executives that an organization may become a magnificent group of specialists (and the larger the company, the greater the specialization) with no one qualified to direct them.[4] Possession of this rare skill depends upon breadth of judgment and understanding, which are exclusively products of experience, and it is unlikely that a man will ever acquire this experience unless special good fortune permits it. No one can become a really efficient general manager under modern conditions until given opportunity and encouragement

[4] Randall, Clarence B., *A Creed for Free Enterprise,* Atlantic—Little, Brown and Company, 1952, p. 133.

to break out of the role of technical specialist and learn how to organize the numerous specialties represented by his organization in a unified team effort.

General administrative or coordinative skills do not depend upon proficiency in each of these numerous technical skills under the generalist's direction. The orchestra conductor need not be a good oboe player or be capable of changing places with the first violin any more than the president of a steel company needs to have first been a metallurgist, a cost accountant, or a blast furnace superintendent.

It is quite likely that either orchestra conductor or chief executive will have, along the way, become reasonably expert in many of the technical skills he directs, long before being trusted with general leadership. But these acquisitions of skill alone are never sufficient preparation for general responsibilities. In fact, one of the commonest errors in choosing general administrators is being too much influenced by the technical specialties of available candidates. Qualification as a superb salesman, a particularly inventive designer, or a brilliant chemist has little actual bearing upon the possessor's chances of success if installed as administrative head of his department.

The care and culture of executives, especially with respect to the general administrative and coordinative skills required of general managers, are frequently far from adequate. In contrast, the formal training in many narrowly technical skills provided by schools of engineering and of business is quite respectable. These schools' graduates almost invariably, after a necessary period of job orientation, are well able to take their place as competent technical specialists in the business community.

Both types of schools, we are frequently told, as institutions of collegiate grade, have fallen far short of the specifications professional educators would like to set for them. Both have been subjected to much unfriendly criticism which, in some instances, is doubtless merited. But, in all fairness, these particular educational efforts need to be appraised on the basis of whether or not they perform an essential educational function and what they can and ought to do within the scope of their restricted objectives and resources.

One of our friendlier foreign critics[5] has reminded us with both envy and admiration that we are the first people to bring higher education not to a tiny élite, but to an enormous slice of an enormous population. This has sometimes been wasteful; some colleges and universities have low standards; many of their graduates are far from being truly educated. This is likely to be true in a country so large and so variegated that it is almost alone as one which has, in a literal sense, put itself to school.

It is too much to expect that more than a very small percentage of the 40,000 or 50,000 graduates in engineering, or of the 30,000 or more turned out each year by our undergraduate collegiate schools of business, will become renowned figures in pure or applied science, eminent industrialists, or business executives entrusted with large affairs. The curricula of both may frequently appear to be not much above the trade school level, but their graduates nevertheless enjoy useful careers—indeed, are irreplaceable—in engineering offices, field sales and customer service forces, and middle management throughout industry. To teach these men to perform functions well may be pure "vocationalism" and, as such, fall short of the proper standards of so-called higher education. But before these enormous and socially essential efforts are condemned too roundly, let us be sure that less wasteful ways have been found to provide preliminary training for the vast army of technicians required—and possibly destined to remain throughout their active lives—in the "noncommissioned" ranks of modern industry.

The alleged deficiencies of undergraduate technical schools are certainly not the most critical problems of education in our times. First-rate executive training has, in contrast, never been very well systematized; indeed, it has too often been left almost to chance. Lack of systematic guidance compels the executive apprentice to rely almost completely upon his own resourcefulness in imitating, or choosing not to imitate, the performance of the imperfect models which he observes or serves as understudy. If the models are deficient and disposed to blunder, is it surprising if later the disciple blunders also when put to similar tests?

With so crude a process by which general executives have

[5] Snow, Sir Charles Percy, British physicist and novelist, in an address at Washington University, St. Louis, in February 1963.

been expected to evolve, the results often could have been much worse. In the large organizations which are so prevalent in our economy, for most executives in training the exposure to narrow specialization tends to be inordinately prolonged. Only relatively late in their business careers, if at all, do many with potential for general managership become eligible to show what they can do.

It is not to be wondered at that many so chosen never prove quite equal to their jobs. It is surprising instead that many do so well with so little systematic preparation.

The Basic Executive Skills

Men who become proficient executives frequently are more indebted to opportunities for liberal or general education than to the curricula of the technical or vocational schools from which they may have been graduated. This is the natural foundation from which the basic executive skills are derived. These special skills can obviously be learned and, once acquired, appear to be readily transferable from one executive environment to another.[6]

The transfer of executive skill has, in fact, been a fairly common experience. In wartime, businessmen have assumed administrative responsibilities in the military forces—if not usually in field service, where special technical qualifications are essential, at least almost universally in the services of supply. The administrative branches of the civil government are always seeking recruits from private business. Retired military commanders have sometimes become successful business executives and government administrators. Educators have been known to serve acceptably as heads of business corporations, and business executives and generals have occasionally become educational administrators with reasonable distinction.

Business consultants, to cite another example, have proved beyond question that basic skills can be transferred to a new environment. Doubtless they are assisted by intellectual detachment

[6] That this is so has been brilliantly demonstrated by T. O. Yntema, Chief Financial Officer, Ford Motor Company, in an address before alumni and guests of the School of Business, University of Chicago, entitled "Transferable Skills and Abilities," in June 1957.

from the local administrative maze which so effectively surrounds their clients, but the fact is that they habitually are faced by management problems which are familiar enough in general outline but embedded in a specific context with which they may have had little prior acquaintance. This novel context does not, however, prevent the competent man from analyzing a situation and finding satisfactory solutions with a minimum of fumbling.

How can this sort of transfer be achieved? Primarily because the distinctive and really essential intellectual equipment of executives is of two basic kinds:

1. *Intimate acquaintance with and understanding of people, mastery of pertinent facts, and familiarity with the local traditions of the specific environment in which the executive operates.* In a new environment this type of knowledge must be re-acquired; the executive requires time to make his adjustment. But ability to re-orient oneself quickly in a new environment is a skill which can be learned, and when learned, is transferable.

   It is the mark of a trained mind to be able to judge new acquaintances promptly, to grasp the correct significance of essential and hitherto unknown data, to put them in proper perspective, to sift out what is irrelevant.

2. *Executive skills embodying principally proficiency in planning, coordinating, and controlling group activities. Planning* processes are universal; the local facts behind the plans need only to be supplied. *Coordination* depends primarily upon skill in working through people. Generally applicable, it too is readily transferable to a new environment. *Control* likewise is a group activity capable of precise definition. It is based on the habit of self-appraisal, on personal dissatisfaction with personal failure, on positive impulses to apply corrective action. If cultivated, these traits readily become habitual, and they invariably depend more upon the commander than upon his troops. The man who has them scarcely need feel ill at ease in any post of command.

This book has made the point that all executives deal with ideas having general application in every business. All deal with things. All deal with persons and their social relationships.

Some leaders, capable of contributions possessing great social value, may be typically thrown in contact more with individuals than with groups. Skill in working with and through groups may seem of little consequence; indeed, the prospect may be viewed with some repugnance by the scientist, the mathematician, perhaps even the surgeon or engineer. It is, however, the very heart of the job of the military commander, the clergyman, the politician, and the business executive.

These variations in vocational interest may possibly affect the emphasis but not especially the substantive content of the educational program by which a cultured personality is developed. The ends of general education which determine curricular means are quite explicit. These aim at liberal cultivation of the mind, manners, and morals of students who will later be expected to serve as community leaders no matter what their institutional workplace proves to be. The necessary qualifications can be stated with reasonable assurance: All educated men, for example, must know how to concentrate, to see and be guided by what they see, to remember, to communicate, to develop self-assurance, to lead an ordered existence, to understand their associates.

Every executive must clearly cultivate the trait of intense mental application. His tasks are arduous. They require prolonged, earnest effort and capacity for personal satisfaction in accomplishment. To work hard and like it is the unfailing secret of success in any worthwhile job. It is an acquired trait, partly dependent upon temperament, certainly upon habit, but more especially upon interest in what one is doing.

Our schools, from kindergarten to university, can hardly be expected to teach or compel mental concentration. But it is education's business at every level to provide challenging intellectual pursuits and, through a rigorous program, to lure students into forming the habit and experiencing the joy of hard mental work and application. That it has not done this very well is one of the common criticisms of our American educational system. The habit of serious reading, for example, unfortunately seems to have little correlation with previous exposure to college training.

To be able to see and to know how to go about solving problems is perhaps the most pervasive and demanding executive skill. It is transferable from one occupational frame of reference to another with almost complete facility. Call it application of the scientific method or what you will, it is at the very root of all creative effort, the unmistakable evidence of disciplined thinking. Proficiency in it requires that one be observant, that one take special note of the minute details of what one sees, that one be able to make use of this previously unfamiliar experience, that one understand the functional relationships of the object under observation, that this newly acquired knowledge be related to what is already known and applied with discernment in new situations.

Mastery of these basic techniques can be promoted by almost any severely intellectual exercise. It is an important by-product of serious practice of the fine arts; of systematic observation and cultivated appreciation of nature; of purposeful study in almost any area—economics, history, language, logic, mathematics, as well as the various branches of biological, physical, and social sciences. This quest, however, is for most students only begun during the period of their formal education. Real proficiency usually is the result of intense application and seasoned experience.

A good memory, of course, is indispensable if these studies are to result in a disciplined intellect. Deliberate attempts to develop the students' retentive powers are customarily not given much attention in formal educational programs. Perhaps they should be given more. That memory is an acquired trait which can be cultivated has been demonstrated beyond question. The rare talents for remembering names, for example, for recognizing faces, and for quickly establishing rapport with newly met associates by relating one's own experience with theirs are distinct executive assets. Actually, these heart-warming personal qualities, dependent upon memory, are frequently much more important than sheer intellectual brilliance in fitting an executive for his prime task of influencing and leading people.

It is self-evident, too, that to think creatively one must have something significant to think about. A mind well stocked with facts, events, and ideas pertinent to pressing issues but not encumbered by the ill-digested trivia which sometimes pass for knowledge is essential. To be without it is to indulge merely in daydreams and wishful speculation. True education and its inseparable companion—wisdom—never depend in particular upon familiarity with specific techniques or processes or upon the accumulation of random information in vast amounts. To recognize and retain that which is relevant to one's purpose is the true test.

Skill in communication quite generally is assigned great importance among the goals of formal education, yet the void between intentions and results is often wide—no one in education seems to be particularly adept at bridging it for the student masses. To communicate lucidly and meaningly—whether in exchanging views, issuing instructions, or reporting progress—is always a two-way operation, involving sending and receiving. Before the process is completed, either between individuals or within groups—before men are ready to act upon what they have received—the utmost ingenuity may be required. Written, verbal, and visual transmission, face-to-face confrontations between individuals, and exhaustive group discussion all may be called into play. Instructions, orders, and background information are seldom acted upon intelligently until the receiver understands perfectly why the desired action is important to the sender.

Communication probably heads the list of executive skills. Organization itself is primarily concerned with designing a structure that will facilitate internal communication. Despite, however, the fact that all effective group effort depends upon it, organization has rarely received much direct attention in formal educational programs. It usually is given a place in the curricula of engineering and business schools, but aside from this (often) not too imaginative treatment, it is an educational discipline recognized more by implication than by direct attack. And perhaps it is better so until educators develop sufficient interest and understanding to prepare suitable materials for instruction in organization theory and practice and to learn how to teach them.

Organizing skills, because of this default, in large part are learned by doing; but, once learned, they are readily transferable to new fields and environments. In any event, an understanding of people and how they contrive to work together—which is the central theme in organization—is essential equipment for the finished executive. It is the mark of a mature mind. It requires the mellowness of spirit and the patience that usually are the product of ripe experience. It requires self-confidence and the ability to engender confidence in others. It depends upon mutual respect, upon integrity, upon warmth of feeling and good humor—indeed, upon affectionate regard of and by one's associates.

This quality of personal leadership which executives must have if their efforts to organize operations are to prove effective is not so much a matter of profound intellectual achievement. It is more concerned with cultivation of the spirit. And those with the sharpest intellect sometimes do not rate very high marks in this important respect.

Business Schools and Curricula

If formal training for executive work must be deeply grounded in what is called general education, what of the further education which, to be of truly professional grade, must be built on this foundation?

Strictly business curricula, for the most part, need to be pitched at the graduate level. Indeed, there may be no alternative if students who have the maturity consistent with professional training are to be attracted.

Undergraduate schools of business have been too greatly handicapped in their struggles to do more than provide their students with introductions to vocational skills in accounting, statistics, salesmanship, or advertising copy writing; some practical applications of economics in business situations; and the like. Executive training at this level is out of the question. There is too big a gap in time and experience between the typical undergraduate's innocence and the personal qualities required in the executive occupations for which business students are supposedly being trained. What executives do has little real meaning to trainees who must wait years before having an opportunity to put what has supposedly been learned into practice.

Some few business schools, perhaps a dozen or so, are attempting more or less competently to cross this void by offering so-called executive training programs. These choose their students among men who have already served their apprenticeship in actual management—who, it is hoped, will be well grounded in their craft when selected by their employers as the "cream of the local crop." Thus they are or ought to be able to make constructive use of this invitation to "go to school again" for a time. In consequence, these truly exciting efforts in advanced adult education can be centered, not upon simple clerical skills, but upon penetrating study involving opportunity for independent investigation of business institutions, functions, and operations. The case method in particular, which originated years ago in the professional schools of law, has equal value in executive training, especially when mature students can be encouraged to develop formal "cases" of their own making.

Courses in characteristic business disciplines like accounting, statistical analysis, law, and economics can in this environment be given a new emphasis. They can focus upon a better appreciation of these specialties by general executives and ways of putting them to work more effectively in solving the business problems of nonspecialists in these technical fields and, conceivably, laying a much firmer base for the expert staff work that is so greatly needed in modern business.

To justify this break in the working life of "marked" men already well launched on successful executive careers demands good teaching as well as good students. A carefully selected class should provide as great a challenge as any teacher could want. But, sadly enough, academic men have learned most of what they know at second hand or by reading each other's books. And inexperienced teachers definitely will not do in education of this distinctly executive type.

Given a fair chance, however, and given the right teachers, these experiments seem likely to prove the best way to integrate formal course work and the informal training absorbed by executive apprentices ,from actual practice. Those concerned with the care and culture of future executives are sure to find in the "back to school" movement, still in its infancy, a useful ally.

Executive Goals and the Future of Free Enterprise

It is not of much consequence, though, whether the returns from this nation's enormous investment in so-called higher education be thought of as liberal, professional, or vocational in emphasis. These are words on which the experts probably may never be expected to agree. What really matters is that all our efforts to educate executives be firmly based on the presumption, once voiced by Winston Churchill, that those who are possessors of a definite body of doctrine and of deeply rooted convictions will be in a much better position to deal with the shifts and surprises of daily affairs than those who are merely taking short views and indulging their natural impulses as they are evolved by what they read from day to day.[7] This cultural standard is obviously something quite beyond the comprehension of those who depend for their intellectual exercise upon television and the chatter of the financial and sports pages of the daily press.

The future of our system of enterprise clearly requires that business executives have a firm commitment—

1. To informed thinking and rational action in the daily exercise of their responsibilities.
2. To serving their customers honestly and well, dealing with employees fairly and with understanding, and looking out for their investors with initiative and prudence.
3. To planning, building, and nourishing the organization in their charge so that it may continue when it is passed on to other hands.
4. To accepting the intelligent citizen's full responsibility for participating in the charitable, cultural, and civic life of the community.
5. To opening wide the channels of opportunity and encouragement, without prejudice, so that all who will may develop their full potential. A civilized community can ill afford to construct barriers against equality of personal and social opportunity.

Under business leaders thus committed, the primary goals of free enterprise and of the free society will have become one.

---

[7] As quoted by Dean Rusk, Secretary of State, in an address before the Academy of Political Science, January 1962.